The California Girl

LISA WOOMER

The California Girl

Lisa Woomer

CITI OF
BOOKS

CITIOFBOOKS, INC.
3736 Eubank NE Suite A1
Albuquerque, NM 87111-3579
www.citiofbooks.com

| Hotline: | 1 (877) 389-2759 |
| Fax: | 1 (505) 930-7244 |

Ordering Information:
Quantity sales. Special discounts are available on quantity purchases by corporations, associations, and others. For details, contact the publisher at the address above.

Printed in the United States of America.

| ISBN-13: | Softcover | 979-8-89391-898-4 |
| | eBook | 979-8-89391-899-1 |

Library of Congress Control Number: _____

CONTENTS

CONTENTS

one

_____

2019

They say everything happens for a reason. Even the bad things. But the reasons for all the things that happened in my childhood still escape me—if only I could have completely escaped the events of my childhood. I have no visible bruises or scars anymore; they have faded to the inside. Those scars are no longer painful, and most of the time I forget I have them. Only sometimes when I come back to visit my mom in the town where I spent my childhood, Grass Valley, California, do I feel them.

I felt them on a recent trip to visit my mother. We decided that it would be fun to take my children to visit a gold mine since my youngest son was about to enter fourth grade. I had visited this same mine when I was in fourth grade. As I watched my children on the tour, looking at their sweet, innocent faces stare up at the giant ponderosa pines towering overhead, I kept flashing back to my own life. I had stood on the same soil covered in a thick layer of pine needles.

We wandered the grounds following our tour guide, my son's small hand in mine, until we finally reached the mouth of the mine; the cool, musty, damp air hit us as we left the scorching midday summer sun. The tour guide told us that during the Gold Rush, gold fell off in flakes, and you could find it everywhere, but then so many people came and picked up all of the free gold that there was nothing left on the surface. It took thousands of men almost a hundred years to mine down several miles into the earth—twenty-four hours a day, six days a week—to find the remaining gold that was embedded in veins of quartz buried deep within the Earth's crust. If a miner had the day shift, it meant that he would never see the light of day. He would get to the mine at dawn and be lowered down, not to return to the surface until dusk. The men would spend the day hunched over, drilling away at the quartz in hopes that they would find a glimmer of gold. They endured these harsh conditions with very little pay because gold was so precious, and gold mining held the possibilities of gaining fortune and ending their suffering.

For so long, I tried to forget. I tried to forget the life that I'd lived here. I tried to forget what I'd learned. I tried to forget what I didn't want to know. I tried to forget what had happened. I buried it deep down and spent my adolescence giving away my gold until there was nothing left. I had to dig deep into my psyche to find the gold again, the real me, the part of me that sparkled and shined so that I could see the sun again. I've found it, and now it's time to tell my story.

two

_____

1983

"Can I go to the bathroom? I think I have to throw up," I said. I didn't want to puke in front of everyone. I had just moved to this school, and people already didn't talk to me. This would just make matters worse.

"You look green. Go to the nurse," Ms. Martin said. Wow, her sensitivity was non-existent. Where had this woman gone to teacher school? Tough Love University? I wasn't looking for a lot of sympathy, but a little *Aw, you poor thing*, or even a simple *Feel better*, would have been nice.

I walked out of the classroom and went straight to the nurse's office. My vision was getting blurry, and I hadn't even grabbed my book bag. The nurse must have attended the same school as my teacher because she sent me home without so much as a *Here, lie down, let me get you a cool towel to put on your forehead.* Nope. Nada. Nothing, just *Go home.*

I'm pretty sure she didn't realize that no one would be there. My mom worked at her new job *all* the time and was hardly ever home. At least she got us a place right across from school. When I finally managed to drag myself across the street, I immediately regretted not grabbing my book bag— which had my house key in it. I would have to jump the dark brown, four-foot-high fence that led to our back patio and pry open a window. I was in no shape to be doing that—my head was throbbing, and I could no longer see at all. I slumped down in front of the door and curled up on the hard cement of the front step.

"Hey, you okay?" a voice said.

I squinted my eyes open and saw a girl with long, wavy, light brown hair standing over me.

"I've been better," I said and tried to sit up without success. "I'm locked out, and I have a headache."

"Happens to me all the time. I mean, the locked out part, not the headache part." She hoisted herself over the fence and landed on the opposite side with a thud. The next thing I knew, she was opening my front door and helping me up.

"What's your name?" I said, trying to focus on her face through the blurry patches over my vision.

"Maeve. What's yours?" she asked as she kicked the door closed with her foot.

"Lindsay Trifling," I said, pointing to the sofas. *Why did I say my last name? That's so lame.*

"Well, Lindsay Trifling, here you go." Maeve plopped me on one of the sofas and disappeared into the bathroom.

I closed my eyes because the light was making everything worse. I probably should have had her take me to my room; my mom would be pissed if I puked on one of her beloved white sofas. She was really proud of those things. She had paid for them on her own with the money she'd made from her fancy new job at a big video game company. She'd done it without the help of my deadbeat dad or her ex-boyfriend that she'd dumped so we could move here and start a new life. I was really trying to be happy here. I didn't want to go back to our old house either, but I kept having these headaches and nightmares here, and I missed my old friends.

"Here ya go. This should feel better," Maeve said, and I felt something cool and damp over my eyes, which startled me.

I grabbed the cool and damp thing and opened my eyes. It was a wet washcloth.

"My mom gets migraines. She's been getting them ever since the divorce. Oh, crap, I gotta go. I told my mom I would be home right after school. Grounded. Got caught cutting school. Bye, Lindsay,"

Maeve said, and then she jumped up, ran out to the patio, and hopped over the fence.

"Bye, Maeve, thank you," I said, but I was pretty sure she hadn't heard me. The nausea had gone away, but my head still throbbed, and it made me tired. I wanted to sleep, but I was afraid I would have another nightmare. I put the washcloth back over my eyes.

When I woke up, I was in my bed, and it was dark out. I had no idea how I'd gotten there; my mom must have put me to bed. I heard the sound of my mom's blow dryer coming from her bathroom. I looked at my clock radio. Six o'clock. Ugh! I did not want to go back to school. My stomach hurt. Maybe I was just hungry. I hadn't had any dinner last night. I rolled over and put my pillow over my head to block out the glaring red numbers on my clock.

"Lindsay, Liiiindsaaaay," my mom said in her singsong-whispery voice she used when she wanted me to wake up.

"Noooo, I don't want to go to school. My stomach hurts," I said, pulling the pillow more tightly against my head.

"You're probably just hungry. I made you some oatmeal." My mom sat on the edge of my bed. "You had another one of your headaches, huh?"

"Yeah."

"Maybe it was a mistake to bring you here. I guess you can stay home today until you're feeling better. I'll call the school." She stood up. "I have to go to work. Promise me you'll eat that oatmeal."

"Thank you," I said and pulled the pillow off of my head. "I will."

She leaned down, kissed my forehead, then left. I waited until I heard the garage door close before I flung the covers off and got up. I felt lightheaded and needed to steady myself before I was able to walk out of my room. I managed to make it to the kitchen, pour some oatmeal in a bowl, and get to the breakfast table without falling over. I took a bite—it was so good, all warm and buttery and brown-sugared.

I heard a knock on the door and froze, waiting. There was silence, and I figured I must have been delirious until I heard it again.

"Lindsay, are you home?" a voice called. "It's me, Maeve."

"Maeve?" I said, standing up and holding onto the table for a moment to steady myself. I walked to the door, looked through the peephole, and saw Maeve's eye staring back at me. I opened the door.

"Hey, you're still in your pajamas. Not going to school?" she said.

"No, my mom said I could stay home," I said.

"That's cool. Maybe we can hang out after school. I'm not grounded anymore," she said.

Wow, she actually wants to hang out with me. "Yeah, sure, okay. I'll see you later," I said.

"'Kay, see you later," she said and turned to walk away.

"Hey, Maeve?" I said.

She stopped and turned back around. "Yeah?" she said, her brow furrowed.

"Thanks for helping me yesterday," I said.

"You're welcome. But you were pretty pitiful, I couldn't just leave you lying there," she said, chuckling as she walked toward the school.

"Yeah, I guess I was," I said as I closed the door. I stood there for a minute, not sure if that had really happened. Did I just make a friend—*finally?*

I finished my oatmeal and spent the rest of the day watching MTV until Maeve came back.

"Here's your backpack," she said when I opened the door.

"Thanks," I said, taking it from her. "Come in."

"You got any snacks?" she asked, walking by me and going straight to the kitchen.

"Um, yeah." I followed her. She already had the pantry door open.

"We have this same floor plan," she said with her head inside the pantry.

"You live in this complex, too?"

"Yeah. Ooh, Cup O' Noodles? Can we make this?" She held up two of them.

"Yeah, okay," I said and felt dizzy as I watched her buzz around the kitchen.

"Yay!" She ripped back the paper lids, filled the cups with water, then put them in the microwave. "Oh my gosh!" She whipped around. "I almost forgot to tell you what happened at school today!"

"What happened?" I sat down at the kitchen table. I wasn't sure I could handle whatever it was she was going to say. I was probably the laughingstock of the entire fifth grade.

"They announced the date for the school dance! Isn't that exciting?" She turned back around to grab the Cup O' Noodles out of the microwave.

"Um, yeah, I guess," I said, but that didn't sound like fun to me at all. I pictured myself standing up against a wall all by myself while other kids walked by, pointing and laughing at me.

"You know Savannah and Georgia? They asked if we wanted to all go together, and then I said we could all have a sleepover at my house after," she said. Savannah and Georgia were two girls in our class that were in my reading group. They were pretty nice, but they always went off by themselves at lunch.

"They asked about me, too?" I said. This was crazy. I didn't think they even knew my name.

"Yeah, we were talking before class, and they said they felt bad for you being sick and everything. So I told them that I helped you after school," Maeve said and put a Cup O' Noodles with a fork in it in front of me.

She talked about the dance and the sleepover and how much fun we were going to have. I sat there and listened to her go on and on about what we were going to do, and my head felt better. I had a friend now—three friends, actually.

The next day and every day after that, we all sat together at lunch and planned what we were going to wear to the dance and what we were going to do at the sleepover. Maeve and I took turns going to each other's houses after school. When the dance finally happened, we didn't end up staying very long, because it wasn't just me—everyone was standing up against the wall not dancing. It was super lame, so we left and went straight to Maeve's house. We devoured the pizza her mom bought us, put on our pjs, and set up our sleeping bags in a circle on her living room floor.

"Should we play Truth or Dare?" Savannah asked.

"Yes!" Maeve said.

Georgia nodded, and I shrugged my shoulders.

"Come on, Lindsay, it'll be fun. We're not going to do anything crazy."

"Okay, I guess," I said. It wasn't really the dare that scared me; it was the truth that I was afraid of.

"Maeve, you go first. Truth or Dare?" Savannah said.

"Dare! Duh!" Maeve said, laughing.

"Okay, I dare you to put a bra on your head and go out in front of your house and yell 'I love pizza' really loud." Savannah said, and we all giggled.

"That is sooooo easy! Hang on," Maeve said and ran upstairs. She came back with one of her mom's enormous bras strapped to her head and posed at the top of the stairway. "How do I look?"

Savannah, Georgia, and I laughed so hard, we were crying.

"Okay, let's go!" Maeve said, running down the stairs and bursting out the front door. We were still trying to catch our breath as we stumbled out behind her. "I LOVE PIZZA!"

We were bent over laughing when Georgia stood up and pointed down the street. "Look, it's the cops!" she said.

"Holy shit! Back inside!" Maeve said, and we all ran back inside her house to the safety of our sleeping bags.

"That was close!" Georgia said, and we all cracked up again.

"Okay, Lindsay, your turn. Truth or Dare?" Maeve looked at me with her eyebrows raised.

"Dare," I said. Ugh! At least I got to choose dare.

"Okay, I dare you to tell us your most embarrassing moment ever!" she said.

"That's kind of like a truth, don't you think?" I said, hoping to avoid talking about anything personal.

"Nope, a dare is a dare, you gotta do it," Maeve said. She rolled onto her stomach and propped her head on her hands, waiting for me to spill my guts.

"Fine, okay, my most embarrassing moment ever. Let's see, hmmm…. Okay, I've got it! It was last month. I started bleeding and thought I was dying. When I told my mom I was going to die, she laughed at me and told me I got my period. I didn't even know what that was," I said, covering my face with my hands.

"Oh my gosh! You already got your period?" Savannah said.

"I haven't got it yet, and my sisters didn't get theirs until they were thirteen. That's crazy! Your mom never had 'the talk' with you?" Georgia said.

"Well, yeah, but she left out *all* of the details. Her version was a magical thing where when a man and a woman—who were married, I should add, she made a big deal about that—loved each other very much, would get together and create a baby, and it would grow in the mother's body until it was ready to be born. The man and the woman would then go to the hospital where the doctor would deliver the baby. So I was totally blindsided when I actually started bleeding. I mean, I didn't know it would be so gross," I said, pretending to gag.

"That's no big deal. It's totally normal. I'm pretty sure Mari already has her period," Georgia said and laughed.

Mari was the only girl in our school with boobs, and they were all pointy and jiggly. All the boys teased her. There was no way I wanted to have giant breasts weighing me down. I did not want to be like Mari. I was terrified because my mom, my aunt, and my grandma all had ginormous breasts that hung down almost to their bellybuttons. I did not want to go through that humiliation, so every night I prayed that I would have small breasts. Kids were brutal, and I didn't want to give them any ammunition to tease me with. Moving here had been hard enough. I'd finally made a few friends, and I didn't want anything to mess that up.

"Yeah, you're probably right. Okay, Savannah, your turn. Truth or Dare?" I said, changing the subject. I hoped they wouldn't ask me any more personal questions; I'd had enough "truth" for one night.

three

———

1984

Maeve and I slept over at each other's houses every weekend after that. It was like we were basically twins: we both had single moms, long wavy hair, braces, and were about the same height and weight.

We were always together until the summer before seventh grade. All of a sudden, Maeve wanted to do crazy things, things she thought made her seem grown up but in reality made her seem childish. She was always trying to get me to shoplift with her. She thought it was fun and exciting. I thought it was stupid and terrifying. She also wanted to start smoking. Her mom smoked.

Her mom was a tall blond who always wore gorgeous, expensive-looking clothing and stilettos, like she was on her way to some important business meeting. She told funny stories and was really nice to me when I came over. She was cool, so I guess Maeve thought smoking was cool, too. I did not; it brought back bad memories that I didn't want to think about. All I could see when I thought of smoking was my evil stepmom hacking away at the kitchen counter, and I wanted nothing to do with it.

These differences between Maeve and I created a rift in our friendship. I'd never forget the day we stopped being friends. We had just returned to her house from the drug store after she went on another one of her shoplifting sprees. We walked into the little outdoor courtyard entrance between her house and her garage. Maeve was already by the front door, but I couldn't move; I was frozen right there in front of the gate.

"Come on, Lindsay," she said. "Don't you want to see what I got?"

No, I really didn't. I just stood there. I realized in that moment that I did not want to be a part of this anymore. I didn't want to do one more thing that didn't feel right. I wanted to feel right, but everything felt wrong. No matter what I did, I always felt like there was a weight on my chest, a deep heavy feeling that made every breath difficult, like I was being buried alive with so much dirt. I was dirty. Why was I letting her make me feel this way? What was I trying to prove? Was I trying to prove that I didn't care about myself? And who was I trying to prove it to? People who didn't care about me? I wanted to forget about my past, about why we had moved here to begin with, and this was making me remember. Maeve wanted to steal and smoke, and I wanted to be law abiding and healthy, I wanted to breathe air. I wanted to be clean. Why was this so hard for me?

I noticed the dirty ashtray next to the step by the front door and the trees leaning in over my head, making a canopy. The sound of the fountain gurgling in the corner and the fluttering of the hot pink bougainvillea petals fluttering across the pebbled cement brought me back to myself. I took a deep breath.

"No, Maeve, I don't want to see what you got!" I blurted out. "And if you don't stop, then we can't be friends anymore."

She looked as if I had slapped her across the face. When her shock wore off, she narrowed her eyes. "I am not going to stop," she said, pulling a pack of cigarettes out of her sweatshirt.

I couldn't believe it, was she really saying this?

"Wow! I guess we're breaking up," I said.

"I guess so," she said, and that was it. I left her house, and we never spoke again.

"What the hell am I going to do now? I just lost my best friend. Friend, huh, I guess I'm using that word loosely. She was never really a friend," I said out loud, trying to convince myself. I sounded like a muttering, crazy person; I needed to think of a plan. I knew seventh grade was going to be torture if I showed up there on Day One as a loner. Junior high kids were like sharks, way worse than elementary school kids. If they smelled a little blood in the water, they'd go in for the kill. I might as well have put a "Kick me" sign on my back right then and there and gotten it over with.

I wandered aimlessly through the townhouse complex, not sure where to go. I walked past my house and out of the complex. I found myself walking toward Savannah's house. Savannah and I were pretty good friends, but not best friends—she already had one of those, Georgia. Even their names made one place, for Pete's sake! Talk about being a third wheel. Savannah, Georgia, and...Lindsay—it just didn't go. I hoped they would overlook that and still want to hang out with me over Maeve, but how could I compete? Maeve was dangerous and exciting. What did I have to offer? A whole bunch of nothing, that's what. I had to appeal to their practical sides. They both came from gigantic church-going families with, like, ten brothers and sisters each, so their parents liked boring, old Lindsay. Since I was apparently on some sort of quest for righteousness, they might appreciate that I was the safer choice.

I walked up Savannah's front steps. When I reached the door, it flew open, and two of Savannah's brothers came flying out, knocking me over.

"Ooh, sorry, Lindsay!" one of them shouted as he ran to the minivan parked in the driveway. "Baseball practice!"

I was on my feet and dusting off my butt when Savannah's mom got to the door, wearing her signature church mom outfit: an off-white mock turtleneck and powder blue polyester knee-length skirt.

"Oh, hi, Lindsay! Savannah's inside with Georgia, they're in her room. Go on in."

"Thank you, Mrs. Barnes," I said. *Great, they're both here, perfect!* I headed down the hallway to Savannah's room and knocked on the door.

"Go away, Jimmy!" she said.

"It's not Jimmy, it's Lindsay."

"Lindsay?"

"Your mom said I could come in," I said as I opened the door.

"Where's Maeve?" she said.

Ugh! Everyone was going to be asking that. I guessed that made sense, it was like being a Siamese twin and showing up with your other half cut off.

Savannah and Georgia were sitting cross-legged on her bed. I shoved over a pile of clothes on the floor and sat on the blue shag carpet.

"That's what I came here to talk about," I said. I took a deep breath. "Maeve and I broke up."

"What?" they both said in unison.

"We broke up," I repeated. Saying it out loud still didn't make it seem real.

"No way, what happened?" Georgia said.

"Well, Maeve and I went to Walgreens, and she took a bunch of stuff again. I asked her to stop, and she flat out said no. I told her if she did it again that we couldn't be friends anymore, and do you know what she said?"

"Ummm, that she wasn't going to stop stealing?" Savannah asked, exchanging looks with Georgia.

"Exactly!" I said and burst into tears, which I did not want to do. They stared at me sobbing on the floor, which made me cry even harder. *Great, they're going to dump me, too. I really am going to be a loner. I should have just gone along with Maeve; this is so much harder than I thought. I mean, what was I thinking?*

I buried my face in my hands and was just about to launch myself into a giant downward spiral, when Savannah said, "Wait, does this mean we can't be friends with her either?"

I stopped crying and looked up. "Uh...," I stammered.

"Oh, thank God," Georgia said, "she always made me nervous anyway."

They both hopped off of the bed and gave me a hug.

four

Summer came and went without much drama until I hit the first day of middle school.

"Oh crap, here she comes," I said to Savannah and Georgia. I had barely stepped foot on the campus of Joaquin Miller Junior High School on the first day of seventh grade, and already I had to confront my nemesis.

"Let's just not make eye contact, and maybe she won't notice us," said Savannah.

"Too late," I said. Maeve and I locked eyes like we were in some weird bullfight. She headed straight for us, and before we could turn and walk away, she was standing there shooting invisible laser beams at me.

"Nice outfit," she said in a tone that made it clear that it was not at all a compliment. She turned to a group of populars, laughing hysterically as if she had just shared some private joke with her lifelong besties.

"When did she become friends with them?" Georgia asked, reading my mind.

"Seriously, we have been broken up for, like, two seconds!" I said.

The gaggle moved on, and we were left trying not to let our jaws hit the ground.

"Ugh, this is going to be a long year! She's so mean! This outfit is awesome, my mom took me to the Esprit outlet in San Francisco and everything. It's totally in!" I said, looking down at my crisp, white, oversized shirt with its short sleeves rolled and collar up, tucked into my bright cobalt blue pencil skirt.

"Don't listen to her, she's just jealous," Savannah said. "You look really cute."

"Thanks," I said, only half convinced.

"Yeah, she probably stole her outfit," Georgia added and gave a snorting laugh.

"She probably did, I wouldn't be surprised. I'm sure all of her new friends think she's soooo cool. Just think, if she ends up in juvy, she'll be legendary," I said.

Savannah and Georgia cracked up, but I had this strange feeling of uneasiness building inside me. I could just picture Maeve in her room digging a needle into a sad-looking Lindsay voodoo doll, throwing darts at my picture, and wringing her hands, cackling with her new friends, casting evil spells and curses on me. Uneasiness seemed to be my feeling of choice those days. I was always feeling uneasy. I always felt like something was off, like I didn't really fit in anywhere. I didn't fit in. I may have looked normal on the outside, but inside I constantly felt like I didn't belong. No matter what I did, the feeling was still there, bubbling, simmering on the back burner. No one could see it but me. It was in a dark, shadowy place, obscured by a smile and a witty comeback—a place filled with whispers and secrets from a past life that my new peers knew nothing about, secrets I was trying to forget. My mind wandered into the darkness.

"Lindsay!" Savannah said, nudging me back to reality. "The bell just rang. Are you okay?" she asked, looking over her shoulder. She and Georgia were already walking away from me toward their first class.

"Yeah, I'm fine," I said, even though I wasn't sure I would ever be fine.

I dug my schedule out of my backpack to double check that I had Modern Dance first period. Yep, still right there, first class of the day, unfortunately. I had just spent two hours perfecting my look, and now I had to change into my dance clothes and undo it all. Well, at least it was the first day of school, so maybe we wouldn't have to change.

Sure enough, the locker room was empty, so I raced toward the classroom. Everyone was already sitting on the floor with their backpacks lined up against the back wall under the ballet bar that spanned the entire length of the classroom.

"You must be Lindsay Trifling," said the tall, graceful-looking woman with dark brown skin. She stood in the front of the room with her face tilted down, peering over her readers to look at me.

"Umm, yes, sorry I'm late. I thought we had to change first," I said, still standing by the door. I heard snickering coming from the corner of the room. I glanced over and spotted Maeve whispering to her new crew. I had an overwhelming urge to bolt out of the room. I didn't think I could bear to be in that class with her all year. I felt my chest tighten and my face turn hot.

"Well, Miss Trifling, glad you could join us. Have a seat. I'm Ms. Johnson." She turned her gaze toward Maeve. "That will be enough."

Maeve stopped talking, stunned, and shot me a look that said, *You're dead*, like it was my fault she was being a jerk. I already loved Ms. Johnson and wanted to run up and hug her, but instead I rushed to an open spot on the floor. Ms. Johnson handed me a syllabus and continued.

"As I was saying, you will be expected to come to class on time, in full dance attire, hair pulled back, no exceptions. We practice only constructive criticism in this class, which means one positive comment, followed by one suggestion. Each class assignment will be given a letter grade. Participation and class assignments will equal thirty percent each, totaling sixty percent of your grade. Your final will consist of a dance that you will choreograph with other class members that will be assigned to you. The finished product will be performed at our recital in May for the entire school. Because it is in May, it is called 'The May.' You will not only be expected to work cooperatively with your classmates to choreograph your routine, but you must also design and come up with your costumes and set decoration."

Ms. Johnson kept talking, but everything was a blur after that. My mind raced; all I could do was think about how horrible it would be if I were paired up with Maeve. Maybe if I talked to Ms. Johnson and explained the situation, she might not put us together. It was a long shot, a risk I wasn't sure I wanted to take. I got a distinct dance-teacher-from-*Fame* vibe—"You want fame, well, fame costs, and right here's where you start paying, in sweat." Seriously, why were dance teachers like that?

I remembered when I was five years old and first started taking ballet and gymnastics at Zelda and Lonnie's Dance Studio. Zelda and Lonnie were a Russian mother-and-daughter duo. They looked exactly alike except Zelda had a gray bun and Lonnie had a black bun, but both buns were pulled so tight, it looked like their eyelids wouldn't close. Anyway, I was learning how to do a somersault on the low non-padded wooden balance beam when I rolled right off, hitting the back of my neck against the sharp right angle of the beam. I, of course, had the misfortune of feeling pain, so I started to cry. Zelda informed me in her heavy Russian accent, "We do not cry in gymnastics. Get up, do again." I remember thinking, *Well,* we *may not cry in gymnastics, but* I *do!* That was the first and last year of gymnastics for me. I switched to tap after that.

I heard the rustling of papers from behind me and noticed that everyone was up and putting their syllabi in their backpacks to leave. Wondering how much I'd missed of Ms. Johnson's lecture as I'd zoned out, I got up, grabbed my backpack, and checked my schedule again.

The rest of the day was pretty uneventful accept that Maeve was in another one of my classes, pre-algebra. As if math wasn't torture enough, I had to endure another fifty minutes of snickering from behind me. Seriously, didn't this girl have anything better to do than whisper behind my back?

She had a new group of friends. She could still have been my friend if she'd wanted to be. Instead, she'd chosen smoking and stealing over me. If I was so boring, you would have thought she would have left me alone. Nope, that wasn't the case, she continued to torment me every single day, and I continued my meager existence: get up, get ready for school, walk to Savannah's house, walk with Savannah to Georgia's house, walk with Savannah and Georgia to school, go to modern dance, get dirty looks from Maeve, go to pre-algebra, get laughed at by Maeve, stand around with Savannah and Georgia to eat a bagel and cream cheese, finish school, walk back home, do homework, mope, eat dinner, call Savannah to see what she was wearing the next day, go to bed.

Life continued like this for almost the whole school year until I had my first big break out of Loserville. Ms. Johnson decided to let us choose our own partners for The May! It was like a gift from God! I couldn't believe it! And, if that wasn't enough, Valerie Thompson asked me to be in her group!

Okay, now I need to back up the story again. In sixth grade, when I was still Maeve's sidekick, we all went to science camp in Santa Cruz. We went on a bunch of nature walks, licked banana slugs (it's a thing there, totally gross if you ask me), and did a bunch of other things that I barely remember. The only thing I remember from science camp—like it happened yesterday—had nothing to do with science: I was popular for two days. How, you ask? A miraculous event occurred on the last night of camp.

We had a dance on Thursday night to celebrate. The boys were all break dancing, so everyone formed a circle around them. A boy would do his move, then point to someone, and then that person would go to the center to dance. One of the boys started doing a move called the "coffee grinder," which I had learned in my tap class.

So I blurted out, "I can do that."

This kid from my math class standing next to me, Jake Kwan, heard me say this and said, "No way, Lindsay said she can break dance." And then he shoved me into the middle of the circle.

Oh crap. I stood there like a deer in headlights, but before I could figure out how to make myself invisible, everyone started chanting my name.

"Lindsay, Lindsay, Lindsay, Lindsay!"

"Come on, Lindsay, prove it!" Jake said.

"Uh, okay," I said, and I crouched down on one leg with my other leg stretched out to the side, my new pink Chuck Taylor high tops in full view, my hands planted on either side of my bent leg. "Here goes nothing," I said, and then I swung my straight leg around and around and around, jumping over it with my bent leg. The faster I went, the louder the cheering got.

When I finally stopped and stood up, Valerie Thompson came running into the circle with a bunch of her friends and hugged me, practically knocking me over again.

"Lindsay, that was awesome!" she said. "We are going to start a girl break dancing group, and we'll all get pink high tops! We can call ourselves the Pretty Pink Poppers!" Valerie and her friends squealed with excitement.

"Okay," I said, still kind of in shock over what had just happened. I felt like I was in a bizarre dream. Valerie put her arm around my shoulder and led me to some benches where I sat with them and listened to their big plans for when we got back to school.

The next day, everyone was saying "Hi" to me and complimenting me as we loaded the bus back to school. That was Friday. I have to admit, it felt great to be noticed by everyone. I was really looking forward to Monday for a change. Then, as quickly as it had started, it was over. The weekend seemed to erase everyone's minds. I mean, I wasn't expecting a parade or anything, but no one said a word to me. It was like it was back to business as usual, where no one talked to me. So much for the sixth grade Pretty Pink Poppers.

Interesting side note, Jake Kwan did ask me to "go with him" the following week, and since I didn't have a bunch of boys breaking down my door to be my boyfriend, I said "Okay." He asked me to go to the movies, and I agreed. My mom dropped me off. Jake and I sat next to each other in silence and watched the movie, then my mom picked me up, and that was the extent of our "going together." Jake and I remained friends after that, though. He was pretty much the only person that didn't have amnesia after science camp and would actually say "Hi" to me in the halls.

Anyway, here I had Valerie Thompson standing in front of me, *speaking* to me, as if she'd suddenly recovered from her amnesia.

"So, Lindsay, you're gonna be in our group, right?" she said.

"Um, yeah, sure," I said, trying to contain my excitement over not having to be in a group with Maeve. The only thing that kept me from jumping up and down and screaming was my mild annoyance at

Valerie's people skills. I mean, she hadn't really asked me so much as told me what to do, but I didn't care. I was in a group, and it didn't include Maeve.

"Awesome! I have the best idea for a routine! It's gonna be so rad!" Valerie said.

"Yay!" I said.

Valerie spent the rest of the class period describing her vision, and when she finally stopped talking, she asked what I thought.

Oh boy, be nice, I had to tell myself. *Say something helpful without changing anything.* "Um, I think we should use glitter when we do the jazz hand circle thing," I said.

"Ahhh, oh my God! That's perfect!" Valerie squealed and hugged me. Then the bell rang, thankfully. I felt drained from all of her energy.

"Well, gotta go," I said, backing out of her embrace.

"'Kay, byeeee!" she said and ran off.

"Byeeee!" I said. *Yikes.*

Six months later, I realized Valerie Thompson hadn't forgotten my slick dance moves after all, because there we were on the stage, together. It actually happened—my brief visit to PopularLand became an invitation to live there permanently. This is how it went down.

With forehead pressed into the stage floor, body curled up in a ball, arms crossed in front of my chest, and hands filled with glitter, my heart pounded so loud I could feel my eardrums thumping. I couldn't believe this day, this moment, was here. I felt the entire school boring a hole in me with their eyes, their faces obscured by the dimmed lights of the gymnasium. The only light streaming in came from the small, vented windows that lined the wall near the ceiling, illuminating the dust particles that floated above the hum of the hushed audience.

I felt like I had to pee. That was impossible because I'd just gone. Out the corners of my eyes, I saw Valerie Thompson and her crew in our matching shiny aquamarine unitards surrounding me in similar balled-up positions. I tried to run through the routine in my mind. Shoot! My mind was drawing a blank. Was it knee up, then arm circle, or the other way around? Ugh! Why did this always happen? I'd finally gotten my big moment there on the stage, in front of the whole school—the whole freaking school!—and there I was, losing my mind. It would be just like sixth grade where everyone forgot that I existed, or worse, they would remember who I was and laugh at me every time they saw me.

Sometimes I wished I was invisible. It would have saved me a lot of grief. If I could just get this right, maybe my life would change. Maybe I wouldn't feel like hiding in the shadows. Maybe I wouldn't have to hide myself. I always felt like I needed to hide. I always felt like I was hiding something. I was hiding my past. I was hiding my secrets.

Sweat beads began to form on my temples and upper lip. I heard the first techno drum beat of A-Ha's "Take On Me." *Oh, crap, here we go.* After two full eight counts—BAM—I was up, arms and knee lifting together, the glitter flying with my giant arm circle, making the jazz hand move. The gym erupted in cheering, clapping, hooting, and hollering. All of a sudden, my memory came flooding back to me. Valerie and I looked at each other, smiling. Feeling energized, I forgot about being nervous and actually started to enjoy myself.

We were about two minutes in when it came— the swirling sound and the big ripple move, followed by more cheering and hooting. We were building up to the big finish: chenne turn, chenne turn, chenne turn, leaping turn, spin, then BAM! We dropped to the floor.

I was breathing so hard I couldn't hear the gym going crazy. My heart was pounding out of my chest. I looked over and saw Valerie running toward me, arms outstretched. The other girls were heading my way, too. Before I realized what was happening, I was in a giant, giggling, stumbling group hug.

Ms. Johnson called out, "All right, ladies, that's enough, take it backstage." Then she peered over her glasses and added, "I will talk to y'all later about the glitter. Next!"

That had definitely been an uphill battle, let me tell you. Getting to dance with Valerie Thompson was the first step on my marathon to becoming a non-loser.

The second step was actually trying out for and making the dance team my freshman year of high school. I had to overcome my propensity to try out and fail. This was easier said than done.

five

———————

1986

As I fiddled with the safety pin, trying to get my number attached to my leotard without stabbing myself, I couldn't help but think back to a year ago at my last try-out. I'd decided to once again risk humiliation and try out for cheerleading after having failed the previous two years. I knew it was a long shot, and guess who did make it? That's right, Maeve. When she started hanging out with the populars, somehow, through osmosis, she made the squad.

I pretty much knew I was doomed to fail as soon as I stepped into the gym and saw her sitting on the floor in her cheerleading uniform whispering into the ear of Kristin St. Johns, the head cheerleader. All of the confidence got sucked right out of me. I went through the motions of the routine with absolute perfection, but the words stuck in my throat and came out more like whispers and squeaks rather than actual cheers. I almost didn't even stick around to see the list posted because I knew my name wouldn't be on it. But of course I stayed. Maybe I was just a glutton for punishment.

When I cried to my mom later that evening, she didn't offer up much sympathy. All she said was, "Well, I guess you didn't want it bad enough." Seriously, that was all she said. I didn't have the energy to explain the dynamics of the junior high political system to her. I was too busy wallowing in my own self-pity.

Maybe she was right, though. Maybe I didn't want to be a cheerleader. Maybe I really just wanted to be a dancer. Plus, with Maeve on the squad, that would mean I would have to hang out with her again. I could just picture it, Maeve and Kristin holding up the megaphone, shouting, "Okay, everyone, time to go in and steal your pantyhose and lipstick, and then we'll all rendezvous back here for a smoke." Um, thanks, but no thanks.

After The May, Maeve seemed to ease up on her Lindsay torment, and since I was no longer the school pariah, I decided to test my luck at trying out for the high school drill team. I know what you're thinking—slinging fake rifles around sounds weird and is not exactly dancing, either. But this drill team was more of a dance team that occasionally marched in parades with the marching band, and there was no gun slinging involved.

At tryouts, I scanned the room and noticed that among the rows of girls in various degrees of stretching, Maeve wasn't there—thank God! I was finally free of her. I had the sudden realization that none of these high schoolers knew who I was. I had a fresh start—better than a fresh start, even, because I'd convinced Savannah and Georgia to try out with me. Georgia decided to try out for the flag team, so she was outside. Savannah was with me, but they alphabetized us, so Barnes and Trifling ended up on opposite sides of the gym.

I, of course, ended up at the end of the line right between, Amanda Tam and Juliet Wu. I was really surprised to see Amanda there. She was the smartest girl in school. The look on her face indicated she'd rather be home working on a cure for cancer than standing around a gym pretending to stretch. I only had one art class with her, so I didn't know her that well. She pretty much kept to herself in the dark back corner of the art room, hiding behind her enormous glasses and her shiny, waist-length, black hair. Come to think of it, I wasn't sure I'd ever heard her speak.

Juliet, on the other hand, was a talker. I didn't know her that well, but she had been in my French class last year. Lucky for her, it was a class that rewarded talking, even if it was in a different language. She was the only one who managed to make the teacher laugh. I mean, it takes talent to be able to pull off jokes in another language. Everything about her was funny, including the fact that she was the only Chinese girl in school with naturally curly hair, which she'd talked about in class one day, in detail and *in French!* Mademoiselle Thomas had been doubled over and practically crying, she had been laughing so hard.

"Hey, Lindsay, need some help?" Juliet said, pointing at my number.

"Hey, Juliet, yeah, thanks," I said. "They don't make these for lefties."

Juliet fastened my safety pin. "I don't think they make them for anyone, I already stabbed myself. There, all set. See, look." She pulled down her leotard, revealing a fresh red gash on her chest.

"Yikes! Sorry I wasn't here to help you," I said.

"Not your fault. I was in the bathroom, nervous pee," she said.

"Oh my God! You have that, too? I always feel like I have to pee before I perform!"

"Yes! Oh my God! We are soulmates! Where have you been all my life?"

We both giggled.

"My mom made me come here," Amanda blurted out.

Juliet and I spun around to look at her, our mouths gaping open.

"Wait, did you just say something?" Juliet said.

"Yeah, my mom made me come here, said it would be good for my college resume," Amanda said.

"I don't know how to dance, but I feel like I have to pee, too."

"Well, that's a good sign," I said, trying to be helpful.

Juliet wrapped her arms around our shoulders and pulled us in for a group hug. "We'll help you! We're three pees in a pod now!"

This sent us into fits of laughter, and all eyes turned toward us.

"*Ah-hem!*" the petite blond girl standing in the front of the auditorium gave a fake throat clear. "All right, girls, I hope you all have your act together because we are starting now."

I would later find out the petite blond girl's name was Chanel Morgan. *The* Chanel Morgan who'd led the Lynbrook High School Valkyries to the state championship last year as a junior captain. In ancient history, Valkyries were the angels that took the Vikings that had been slain in battle up to Valhalla, the Viking Heaven. I'd had no idea when I tried out for the drill team that I was stepping into a decades' old tradition that required a history lesson and a test! I'm not kidding, we had to take a written exam in addition to the physical audition in order to make the team. They also made my mom sign a letter that promised she would volunteer for the Valkyrie boosters. This was some serious stuff.

Chanel Morgan was now the senior captain and was not going to stop until we got to Nationals. I have to admit, I was a little unsure of what I was getting myself into at first, but wasn't that what I wanted? I wanted to belong to something. I wanted people to care if I showed up or not. I wanted to spend every last moment dancing. Here it was, the opportunity of a lifetime. According to my mom, all I had to do was *want it bad enough*. So there I was, making sure I was there every day that week, learning choreography and practicing until I couldn't move anymore. Until finally the day of the actual audition finally came:

"Okay, numbers twenty-five, twenty-six, and twenty-seven, you're up," said a voice from the long table of judges at the front of the room.

Holy crap, that was us. I stepped up to the middle x marked in black masking tape on the industrial tiled floor of the practice gym, between Amanda and Juliet. My heart felt like it was pounding out of my chest, and it took all of my muscle strength to hold myself still in the opening position: parade rest, feet shoulder-width apart, arms bent at the elbows, hands overlapped at the small of my back, chin down. The first count of the fight song played, "Bam", and I snapped my head up to face the judges and started my first eight count of pony stepping while doing a circular clap, then pony knees with cross diagonal arms first punching down then up right, then two arm circles right into an exhausting two full eight counts of high kicks, then pas d' bourree, pas d' bourree, double pirouette, pas d' bourree, pas d' bourree, double pirouette, bend, slide right, slide left, bend, and hit ending pose. Phew!

Next up was a custom Chanel Morgan routine to the Salsoul Orchestra's "Magic Bird of Fire." My body went on autopilot because I had practiced the routine a thousand times. The whole thing was a blur, and then it was over. All I could do was wait—wait to see if I'd get to stay in PopularLand or be shunned back to Loserville.

The minutes felt like hours. I felt angry and impatient waiting for the clock to move its hands. They were so slow. I paced. I couldn't stand it. I wanted to climb up the wall, rip off the clock, and smash it on the ground.

"Oh, for God's sake, Lindsay, sit down. You're making me nervous," Savannah said.

I ignored her and continued on my path. It was the only thing keeping me sane while I waited.

"What's with *her*?" Georgia walked in and sat down on the gym floor with Savannah.

What's with me? What's with me, she asks? I shouted in my own head. What was with me was that if I got yet another rejection, I would totally lose it! I had been more than calm my whole life, sweet and nice, never complaining.

My mind went back to the scary time in my life before we'd moved. I pushed the thoughts out of my head. *No, you are not welcome here.* My mom had decided to move hundreds of miles away so that *she* could start over—excellent, super, whatever. I'd tried to make the best of it and tried out for cheerleading three times and *failed* three times, totally awesome!

Well, that was it! I was done being nice. I was going to start taking what I wanted and not be sorry about it. I wanted to start over, too! I was going to pace until there was a frickin' groove in the floor. I was going to will the judges to choose me with the sheer power of my mind.

I mean, really, my mom had said the last time I'd tried out that I must not have wanted it bad enough. Well, this time I wasn't going to let that happen. I wanted to make it so bad. It was like I was possessed or something. I had been practicing like a maniac—in the shower, while I was eating, while I walked to and from school. Even in my bed at night I ran through the routines over and over in my head. Nothing would stop me.

I noticed out of the corner of my eye everyone else getting up and running toward the office windows. I stopped in my tracks, turned my head, and saw The List posted on the glass. There it was. My body took over on instinct and ran toward The List; I leapt over backpacks and shoved through the crowd. I was locked-in, now in *Terminator* style, while I scanned The List.

And there, at the bottom, I finally saw it in Arial bold font:

Lindsay Trifling.

That's my name! I made it!

My ears went numb. I saw girls hugging each other and laughing, but I couldn't hear them. Everything seemed to be happening in slow motion. I felt light-headed. I leaned back on the wall for support, but my legs gave out, and I slid down the wall to the ground.

"Lindsay, Lindsay, are you okay?"

I heard a muffled voice and looked up. Savannah, Georgia, Juliet, and Amanda were all staring down at me with furrowed brows and their hands on their hips. The blood returned to my brain, and I managed to speak.

"Um, yeah, I think so," I said.

"We made it! Aren't you excited?" Georgia asked, reaching for my hands to pull me up.

"Yeah, I just can't believe it!" I said.

"Come on, Lindsay, you practiced that routine about a million times. There was no way you weren't going to make it, and if they didn't pick you, I would have had to kick some butts!" Juliet said and did a high roundhouse kick. This sent Savannah, Georgia, and me into fits of laughter.

"Thanks. They must have some tall butts," I said.

"I made it, too!" Amanda said, which made us pause in our laughter.

"Wow, that's awesome! Congratulations!" I said.

"Well, I didn't make the drill team, exactly. I made the mascot squad. I get to wear one of the Viking costumes at all the games," Amanda said.

"Wow, that's still awesome!" I said and gave her a hug.

Juliet, Savannah, and Georgia joined in. That was how it happened. The five of us were inseparable after that. We were the Fantastic Five. People would high five us in the halls after seeing us perform at games. We were famous, and not just for being cute or rich, but for actually having talent and winning every competition we entered. We literally spent every minute together. We practiced, ate, and did homework together.

We were a team, and *the* Chanel Morgan's dream came true. We made it to Nationals all the way in Florida. We put on our matching navy-blue-and-white Adidas warm-up suits that had "Valkyries" written in cursive on the back and marched through the airport. I felt like a celebrity as everyone turned to look at us. And we won! Well, we got third place, but that was still amazing for our first time there, and Chanel Morgan got to stand on the podium just like a bronze medalist in the Olympics and hold up a ginormous trophy.

Life was amazing! I hardly ever thought about my old life before we'd moved to San Jose. I didn't have any migraines or bad dreams anymore. Even my mom had met someone at work and started dating him. His name was Chip, and he came over a few times. I liked him. He was funny. He liked to crack jokes, but to be honest, I didn't get to know him too well because, like I said, I was always with the Fantastic Five. So it felt a bit like I'd been stabbed in the heart and had the air sucked out of my lungs when my mom sat me down and told me she was getting married to Chip and that we were going to be moving in with him at his house near their office in Redwood City.

"Doesn't he live an hour away?" I said. My mind was calculating the distance and trying to figure out how they were planning on getting me to school—because if there was one thing I knew for sure, it was that I was not changing schools again. No way, no how.

"Uh huh," she said with a smile on her face. How could she have been smiling at a time like that?

"So am I going to live with Grandma and Grandpa again?" I said, feeling thankful that they had moved back to San Jose about six months after we had.

"Um, no. You'll live with us. Chip can drive you to and from school for the rest of the year since he has an office at the San Jose airport, but then next year you will transfer to a school closer to Chip's—I mean, *our*—new house," she said.

And that was it. She had made another decision that I had no say in. My life in PopularLand was over as quickly as it had started. I was moving back to lonely Loserville again.

I will spare you the gory details of my fifteen-year-old rage fit that followed this little convo, but let's just say it took a good solid forty-eight hours before either one of us spoke to each other again. It was ugly. The only good thing that came out of this was that I got my braces off. So at least I wasn't starting a new high school as a brace-faced loner. I was just a loner.

six

———

1987

It was the first day of sophomore year at a new school, and I was standing in the P.E. line to get my P.E. uniform alone. P.E., ugh! If I were at my old school, I would have been in dance class for drill team, not P.E. The thought of starting all over again was almost too much to handle, but I was trying to make the best of it. I mean, there were some good things about moving. It meant that my mom didn't have to commute anymore *and* actually made dinner for me *and* we sat down *and* ate it at a table. It was a nice change from me coming home to an empty house, heating up a can of Chef Boyardee, and eating in my room while doing homework.

Anyway, soon enough I was standing around the dank locker room during P.E. class next to some chatty girls in pastel-colored cashmere sweaters, trying to ignore the faint smell of mildew. One of the girls was leaned up against a rusty, pale blue locker, talking about how her parents were in Europe for the rest of the month and how she was going to throw a rager that weekend.

Another girl burst out laughing and said, "Remember how wasted we got last time?"

This caused them all to double over in laughter. When they settled down, the owner of the empty house noticed me standing there and said, "Hey, what's your name?"

"Lindsay," I said

"Love your top. You should come," she said, and she grabbed the syllabus out of my hand and wrote down her address.

"Thanks," I said, and then the P.E. teacher told us to line up to get measured for our P.E. uniforms.

During the shuffle, I was separated from the cashmere sweater club and found myself behind two dark-haired girls wearing denim jackets. One of the girls was bouncing around in line, singing to herself.

"Lainey, cut it out," I heard the other one say.

"What?" the singing girl said, and then she saw me standing behind her and stopped. "Oh, sorry."

"That's okay," I said.

"Hi, I'm Lainey, and this is Anna." She stuck out her hand for me to shake.

"Hi, I'm Lindsay." I shook her hand.

"You're new. Where are you from?" she asked.

"Um, I'm from San Jose," I said, not wanting to get into the whole history of places I'd lived and where I was actually "from."

"Oh, cool. Hey, do you want to hang out at lunch?"

"Sure, thanks," I said, maybe a little too eagerly. I did *not* want a rehash of my loner days, and having lunch with other girls would help me steer clear of Loserville.

"Awesome! I thought you might already be going to hang out with April Vanderslut."

"Lainey!" Anna said, shoving her in the arm. "Don't listen to her, it's Vanderpoole."

"Uh, no. She just wrote down her address for some party she's having this weekend," I said.

"I'm so glad I saved you from that. You *do not* want to get involved with the trust-fund crew," Lainey said. "They have all this money, and their parents are never around, so they do whatever they want, and when they get busted for doing drugs, their parents just write a big fat check, and it all just disappears," she said, making a circular gesture with her hands.

"Wow!" I said.

"Ohhh, I'm so excited to have a new friend!" Lainey said, flapping her arms. "Can I dip you?"

"What?" I said. Did she just ask if she could dip me?

"You might as well let her, it's gonna happen anyway. This is what she does," Anna said.

"Okay, fine. Dip me," I said.

"Yes!" Lainey said and proceeded to dip me.

We both laughed.

"Well, that was a lot more fun than I thought it was going to be," I said.

"Hey, girls, you're holding up the line," the teacher said, leaning over the wood-and-metal folding table where the uniforms sat.

"Oops, sorry, Mrs. V," Lainey said as she stepped up to the table.

"Yeah, yeah. No more funny business," Mrs. V said.

What I would later learn was that Lainey was *all* funny business. She saved me from a lonely high school existence. I mean, if you could have friendship at first sight, that was what we had. We just clicked instantly. It was like we had been separated at birth or something. Well, she was Japanese, and I was Italian, Irish, Portuguese, and a mix of a bunch of other European ancestry, but still, we were friend soulmates.

She introduced me to Anna and Jess, and we formed a new group, the Fabulous Four. I knew we were going to be lifelong friends when Jess let us call her *Jess* instead of *Jessica*. She was particular about who she allowed to use her nickname; if someone tried to call her Jess who was not a close friend, she would correct them: "Um, it's Jessica."

We did everything together—we met up at break time, at lunch, and on the weekends. Since I didn't have any practice to go to, we basically spent every weekend having rotating sleepovers at someone's house. Anna was a little older than us, and she got her license first. She also got a car, a white convertible Carman-Ghia. It was spectacular, and we would drive around in it like we were in a movie, waving our arms in the air and singing at the tops of our lungs with our hair flowing in the breeze.

Nothing separated us; not even my string of random boyfriends could break up the Fab Four. I don't know what it was—my hormones, getting my braces off, being new blood at school, or a combination of all three—but I was like a dude magnet by the middle of my sophomore year. All of a sudden, boys were paying attention to me. It seemed like everywhere I went, I met a guy, and five minutes later, we would be making out. Okay, maybe not *five minutes later,* but within forty-eight hours, for sure.

I met this guy at the bus stop, and the next day he followed me home and we made out. This was actually a little traumatic because my mom and stepdad came home, and I was playing music so loud that I didn't even hear them come in, so they were probably standing there watching us smooch and grope each other on the sofa for a good five minutes. We were all mortified. My stepdad drove the poor kid home, and I was basically grounded for the rest of my sophomore year. But to be fair, I introduced Anna to another guy I met on the bus, and they became a serious couple right away, so it wasn't just me hooking up with random guys at bus stops.

Anyway, I did manage to kiss a few more boys that year. There was also the boy that asked me to "go with him" from my English class, Garret Lindstrom. Garret and I "went together" for about two weeks until the first school dance. We both realized that we would be better as friends since when we kissed, it was like kissing our hands—no spark at all.

Then I met the boy from Taco Bell and the boy from across the street. They were both two years older than me. I was kind of torn between the two, so I never fully committed to being "boyfriend and girlfriend" with either one of them. The Taco Bell guy was super responsible and nice—I mean, he had a job and everything. The guy from across the street was kind of a flake, but he seemed mysterious and dangerous and would leave notes for me in the bushes. The guy from Taco Bell and I actually ended up being really good friends, and we went to his senior prom. Then he graduated and went off to join the Navy. We kept in touch that year by writing letters to each other. It was kind of like having a pen pal. When he got home from boot camp, he asked me to marry him. I'm not sure if it was because I was the only female he had been in contact with for the past year while he was surrounded by a bunch of other lonely guys, but I was completely caught off guard. I actually thought he was kidding at first because, seriously, I was only sixteen years old. I didn't even have a driver's license yet. That was when I had to let him down easy—but it wasn't easy. It was awful. I felt horrible, but it had to happen. I was too young, and we both knew it.

I knew I needed a distraction, so that summer after my sophomore year I decided to get a job. But, like I said, I still didn't have my license even though I had turned sixteen in January. My mom said I wasn't ready. I actually think *she* wasn't ready for me to have that kind of freedom. Anyway, my lack of a license didn't stop me from getting a job near our house at the frozen yogurt shop, Yogurt Obsession.

Yogurt Obsession, aaaaaaah! Cue the angelic music and heavenly lights shining down on the little white cinderblock building in the Lucky's grocery store parking lot. I was completely obsessed with Yogurt Obsession. I loved everything about it—the sweet vanilla smell of fresh waffle cones, the array of bright-colored candy and fruit toppings in neat rows behind the shiny glass partition, the way the soft serve machine made perfect yogurt kisses into tiny paper sample cups, the crisp black-and-white checkered floor—everything!

When I first stopped by for the job, they weren't hiring, but that didn't stop me. I rode my bike there every day and kept asking them to hire me. I think I finally wore them down because one day, after serving me my fifth white pistachio in a waffle cone cup of the week, Jeff and Kathy, the owners, agreed to hire me. At this point, we were on a first-name basis. They were a cool young couple—or at least, they wanted to be. When I tried to call them Mr. and Mrs. Turner, they would say, "No, no, call me Jeff/Kathy."

"Can you start now?" Jeff asked, handing me an application.

"Yes! Can I use your phone? I just need to let my mom know," I said, and that was history.

I worked almost every day that summer, learning the ins and outs of the yogurt biz, the joys of mixing flavors into the big machines, and the sorrows of having to clean them out at closing every night. I perfected my swirl and knew just how much yogurt to put in each size cup to still have room for the toppings. I was so excited when I got my first paycheck, I didn't even care that they took out taxes and social security. Honestly, I think I would have done that job for free. They could have just paid me in yogurt, and I would have been happy, but I had my own money, and it was awesome!

I finally got my license at the end of that summer and was able to drive myself to work. One night, the boy from across the street came into the shop right before closing and somehow convinced me to go cruising with him after work. That was my first big mistake. My second was not calling my mom to let her know I was going to be late. The way my mom reacted when I got home was liked I had robbed a bank or something. She basically put me on a work-release program. I was grounded for the rest of the summer and was only allowed to go to and from work. The only good news was that she couldn't stop my friends from visiting me at work, so at least I got to see them. But that was stressful, too, because I really loved my job and didn't want to lose my only freedom, and let's just say unsupervised teenagers hyped up on sugar can get a little rowdy. Most of the time I ended up kicking them out.

The job came to an abrupt end when school started because Yogurt Obsession went back to regular fall hours, and with school and pom pom squad practice, I couldn't fit it into my schedule anymore. Bye-bye, Yogurt Obsession....

seven

1988

Junior year was actually pretty awesome. I had missed being on the drill team so much. Even though my new friends were amazing, I still felt like something was missing. My new school didn't have a drill team or even a marching band—they only had a pep band. When I found out that they had a dance team called the pom pom squad, I wanted in. They were having tryouts at the end of May, so I went to the clinics every day after school to learn the routines, and in true *Lindsay-you-have-to-want-it-bad-enough* form, I practiced like a maniac. I drove the Fab Four a little crazy, making them watch me practice and critique each and every run-through. But it worked! I made the squad!

At that point, not only was the Fantastic Four still going strong, I was on the pom pom squad, *and* we all had our driver's licenses. Well, except Jess, who was a year younger than us, but it was fun to alternate who got to drive to lunch. Well, really, it was just Anna and me alternating because Lainey was frightening behind the wheel. She had so much energy that it was hard for her to sit still and focus long enough to drive, and let's just say her lane changes were way too abrupt, my heart could barely take it.

I got to experience her driving techniques firsthand because we took Driver's Ed classes together. I am surprised I survived that class because between her and this guy named Eddy Wetchie, I thought we were all going to die.

Eddy was not a big talker; he sat in the back of the classroom with his one-inch-thick glasses and black spiky hair and his head down all the time. One day, our teacher took us out to practice driving in one of those cars that also had a brake on the front passenger side. It was Eddy's turn to drive. Lainey and I were in the backseat and were totally unprepared for what happened next. Mr. Madson, who was also the band director, asked Eddy to take his foot off the break and *gently* press the gas pedal to ease out onto the road. Well, Eddy must have been hard-of-hearing because he jammed his foot on the gas with all of his strength, causing the engine to rev like we were about to drag race. Thank God Mr. Madson had not yet released his foot from the brake, or we would have driven right off a cliff or something. Lainey and I hugged each other for dear life. When I looked at her, she was as pale as a ghost, and I must have looked the same.

Anyway, I always felt safer if either Anna or I were driving, not Lainey. I remember the time when Lainey, Anna, and I all pulled into the school parking lot at the same time one morning. Lainey bounced out of her car and gave us giant hugs. She was so excited that she forgot to turn her car off even though she'd remembered to lock the door. Lucky for her, I had to go back out to my car later that day to get a cassette tape for the dance I was performing during the lunchtime pep rally. When I went out to my car, I heard some faint music playing. I tried to figure out where it was coming from and realized it was Lainey's car, which was still running! I tried the door handle to see if I could turn the car off, but the door was locked. I laughed out loud, thinking back to our morning greeting—if anyone would do this, it would be Lainey. I grabbed my tape, made sure to lock my door, and ran back to class. I burst through the door, and the Zen atmosphere of the art room broke as I tried to get out the words while gasping for breath and laughing hysterically: "Lainey, your car is running!"

Everyone looked up from their projects and froze.

"Lindsay, shut up! It is not. Ha, ha, very funny," Lainey said.

I regained most of my composure and said, "No, I swear to God! I'm not kidding."

The whole class erupted in laughter. Mr. Jansen told everyone to quiet down then dismissed Lainey to check on her car.

It turned out Lainey's dad knew her pretty well, too, because he'd put a magnetic key holder with an extra key in it under the fender for just such an occasion.

eight

Since making the pom pom squad, I had built up some confidence. It normally wasn't my thing to just hunt down a guy and ask him out, so I'm not sure what came over me the next day. This cute boy walked into the classroom with his blue eyes and sand-colored hair peeking out from the black-and-red cap all ASB students were required to wear when on duty and interrupted the doldrums of my algebra class. If a Ken doll had a human model, he was it. His presence snapped me out of my meditative state and plugged me in; every cell in my body was coursing with electricity. *Who is this godlike creature, and why have I not seen him before?* I decided that it would be my next mission in life to find out.

He took ten glorious steps toward Mr. Bland and jutted his tanned arm out to hand him a note. Mr. Bland adjusted his glasses and took the note. Mystery Boy put his thumbs in his jean pockets and looked out at the class. And then it happened—our eyes locked. My face felt hot, and the pencil in my sweaty palms slipped to the floor. I looked at the floor and reached down to retrieve my pencil, and when I sat up, he was gone. Holy crap! I looked at the clock—only one more minute until the bell would ring. Thank God! I shoved my binder and book into my backpack.

"Mizzzz Trifling, you have not been excused," Mr. Bland said.

My mind was already out the door. "Um, what?" I said.

"I said you have not been excused yet."

The bell rang.

"Sorry, Mr. Bland, um, it's just there's, uh, pep rally, uh, practice. I gotta go," I said and hoisted my backpack on to one shoulder to squeeze my way through the narrow aisle between the desks. Soon, I was in a full-blown run out of the classroom. Without knowing why, I felt the need to stalk the mystery boy. But by then, everyone was pouring out of their classrooms, and the mystery boy had disappeared into the crowd.

"Hey, Lindsay!"

I heard my name being called and spun around. It was Lainey. I was so relieved to see her. I needed to talk to someone about my new obsession. She was the perfect person to talk to as she had been pining away for Darren Yanaguchi for the past six months, plus she had a knack for cheering people up and making you forget about your problems.

She was running toward me pretending to be in slow motion with her arms outstretched like we were in some cheesy movie. Playing along, I also began my slow motion run toward her, and when the moment finally arrived where we met, she gave me a giant hug, which of course ended in a dip.

While we were in this movie embrace, I said, "Lainey, I think I saw the love of my life today!"

"What? No way? Who was it?" she said and stood me back up.

"I have no idea, but I am going to find out, and he will be mine," I said.

"You go, girl! Hey, maybe we can go on a double date if Darren ever gives me the time of day," Lainey said.

"Okay, deal! But I need you to do me a favor."

"A favor? I'm not sure I like the sound of that." Lainey put her hand to her chin in thinking mode.

"Oh, come on, it's not that bad. I just need you to go into the office and find out who he is," I said.

"So you want me to just waltz in there and start asking around? That's not conspicuous or anything." She rolled her eyes.

"Um, well, yeah. Oh, wait!" I ran over to the rail by the stairs where I saw a sweatshirt hanging. "Here, take this. Tell them you're looking for the lost and found. Then, you can start asking people's names.

He's tall, with sandy blond hair and blue eyes. Here, take it, now go!" I handed her the sweatshirt and motioned toward the office.

"Okay, fine, but you are basically describing half the people here," she said, then snatched the sweatshirt out of my hand and started walking away.

"Don't worry, you'll know when you see him. He'll be the one with the smoldering good looks and the expression on his face that says, *I am super smart but want to seem cool*," I called after her.

She raised her arm up, facing her palm toward me without turning, and said, "Still not helping."

I paced back and forth. The suspense was killing me! Break would be over in five minutes, so I decided to meet Lainey at our next class. Luckily, we had art together, so I would be able to get the low-down from her then. The wait was excruciating. I slid into my chair in the art room and stared at the clock. The first bell rang. *Come on, Lainey, where are you?* She had three minutes until the tardy bell would ring. I literally could not stand it. It seemed like the clock had stopped. I watched the second hand, willing it to move. Finally, with twenty seconds to spare, Lainey came bounding into the room and slipped into the chair next to me. She was breathing hard and trying to catch her breath but still managed a smile. I looked at her, appreciating how quirky she was, and waited for her to catch her breath.

"Well, what did you find out?" I said.

"Oh my God, Lindsay, you were right, he is soooo cute!" she said.

"And?" I said.

"Well, his name is Bill Warner, and he's a senior."

"Bill Warner, that is such an old man name!"

"Yeah, that's what I was thinking, and get this, he's on the golf team! So, technically, he *is* an old man." She laughed, holding her hand over her mouth.

"Wow! I can't believe you were able to get all that info so fast! You're amazing!"

"Well, you might not think I'm so amazing after I tell you what happened next."

"Go on."

"Um, I may have, kind of, sort of, told him that you liked him," she said.

"WHAT?" I said. "No, Lainey, you didn't!"

Mr. Janson was now staring at us and giving us the you-better-stop-talking-or-else-detention look.

We both slunk down in our seats and covered our mouths to continue talking.

"Well, I had to. He wasn't going to answer unless I told him. But there is good news," she said.

"What could possibly be good about that? It's totally humiliating!" I said in an angry whisper.

"Um, he knows who you are, and he likes you, too."

I was flabbergasted at that point and sat there staring at the table. My mind was racing. *How can this be? Where did he see me? We don't have any classes together. Why have I not seen him before?* The questions just kept coming, my mind unable to process any of it, and then I felt a nudge on my arm.

"Earth to Lindsay! Come in, Lindsay!" Lainey said.

"What?"

"Where did you go just now?"

"What? Wait, did he say how he knows who I am?"

"Yeah, he said he saw you shaking your little tushie during the back-to-school pep rally," Lainey said and laughed, covering her mouth again.

"He said that?"

"Well, not those exact words, but...."

"Okay, that's kind of embarrassing. I'm like some peacock, fluffing my feathers to try to woo the opposite sex," I said. Maybe my mom and stepdad were right—maybe I was becoming one of those ditsy girls that only cared about boys and lipstick and shoes.

"Well, technically, I think it's the male that fluffs it's feathers to attract the female."

"Whatever, I was just hoping that I could use my mind to get a boyfriend this time."

"Come on, Lindsay, we barely squeaked by with B-minuses in geometry last year, and he was probably in astro-physics or something. Plus, he can't see your mind before he talks to you," she said.

"Yeah, I guess you're right. So, what should I do?"

"You should totally ask him out."

"Seriously, that's so April Vanderslut," I said and saw Mr. Jansen walking toward us. I gave her the cut signal with my hand.

"Well, she always gets what she wants," Lainey said, not noticing Mr. Jansen was standing over her.

"You know what I want? I want you two girls to quit yapping and get to work," he said.

"Sorry, Mr. Jansen," Lainey said.

"Yeah, sorry," I said.

"Okay, I have a stack of detention slips over here, and I'm not afraid to use them."

"We promise we'll be quiet," I said, and he walked away, still giving us the *look*. I focused on my project sitting on the table in front of me. Without turning my head, I whispered to Lainey out the corner of my mouth, "We'll talk about this later."

nine

It turns out that Bill Warner and I didn't have that much in common other than that we both thought the other was cute. He was brilliant and got a sixteen thousand or whatever on his SAT, and I on the other hand was average, earning the sympathy score on the SAT they give for just putting your name on it. Not exactly a match made in heaven, but it was fun for a while. He was pretty funny in a dry humor sort of way. He would send me clever little notes in class because he was in ASB and could deliver notes right under the noses of the teachers under the cover of "office business." One time, he sent me a poem on Valentine's Day with a rose when everyone else was sending carnations. It said:

> A rose is a rose,
> Is a rose,
> But a carnation
> Is an instant breakfast drink.

He would send me notes after school a lot because we were both really busy with practice and homework and friends.

Hi Lindsay,

I guess you stayed late, huh? Some JV person said you wouldn't be long, so I thought I'd give it a shot, but oh well. Give me a call when you get home. Ok? Merci...

Love, Bill

P.S. – Whose idea was it to bend over and flash the other sideline? We looked just in time to catch that move. Pretty Slick, nice view of seven or eight pairs of red underwear.

He wrote me another note after our failed "egg baby" experiment. I think he felt bad about it and was trying to make up for it. In this experiment, we had to carry around an egg baby all week. Some people took it pretty seriously and dressed up their eggs and made cute little baskets for them, and others didn't—they just shut them in their lockers and left them there the whole week. Well, I was one of those who dressed the egg up and put it in a cute little basket, and one day I thought it would be funny if Bill Warner, a.k.a. the egg baby's daddy, babysat "our" egg baby, Bill Warner, Jr. It turns out that was a horrible idea. Bill Warner had golf practice and put Bill Warner, Jr., in his locker, forgot that he was in there, and squashed him with his backpack.

Lindsay,

Hi Cutie! How's it hanging? No, forget that question. I didn't have anything to do here, and I started thinking about you. So I got this incredible idea that I'd write you a note.

You do that to me a lot you know. Distract me in class, that is. I guess I can't help it. And it's not your fault that you're sexier than most of my teachers. Ok, I admit it. You're sexier than all of them. It's a good thing that you like me because if you didn't, I'd have to sneak looks at you. I hope you don't spend too much time at work this summer. Maybe it'll be some of the time I'm working too. That would be nice. Then we'll have time to spend together. (Sounds like something from Leave it Beaver) Just think, no more school nights. Anyway – nothing special to tell you. Just that I'm thinking about you now and that I will be when you are reading this too.

I love you,

Bill

We went to the prom, and that was fun. The main highlights of the evening were as follows:

*My friend Jeanie from the pom pom squad went with one of Bill's friends, so we rented a limo before the prom and an Embassy Suites room for the after party together.

*Someone scored a bottle of champagne but forgot to score champagne glasses, so we took turns swigging from the bottle.

*Jeanie's date swung his arm around to put on the jacket of his tux just as Jeanie was taking the last swig of the champagne and chipped her tooth.

*After twenty minutes of making sure Jeanie was okay, we entered the prom.

*We danced. A lot.

*We were sweaty, so we left.

*We took the limo to the grocery store to buy chips and cookie dough.

*We went to the Embassy Suites hotel and tried to bake cookies, but the oven didn't work, or we couldn't figure out how to work it, so we ate raw cookie dough and then passed out from sheer exhaustion.

*There were beds, but apparently we just dropped where we were standing because when I woke up we were all sleeping in random spots of the floor.

After the prom, Bill got super busy with college applications, and we started to drift apart. He was going away to college, and I wasn't interested in a long-distance relationship. I was a little sad about it, but in all honesty that relationship had run its course, especially since it was based on superficial physical attraction. I think he started to get tired of having to explain protests in Tiananmen Square to me, and I got tired of being belittled for not knowing what he was talking about. I knew that we needed to break up, but I wasn't ready to do it just yet. I wanted to wait until the summer because we were just too busy. He was always playing golf or studying, and I was always at cheerleading practice or at work, so we didn't get to see each other that much.

When we only had one month until school was out, Mr. Bland moved my seat in front of the cute dark-haired boy across the room, so I was pretty happy. I thought it was innocent enough—I mean, I was just sitting near him in algebra class, what was the harm in being friendly? How was I supposed to know that this change of my seat would actually change the course of my entire life?

I plopped my backpack on the floor next to my new desk and slid into the seat. It was one of those chair/desk combos with the tiny kidney-shaped joke of a desktop. I loathed these with a passion, seeing that I was left-handed, and they were always on the right. It felt like a personal attack, trying to make my life miserable. As I looked up at the board to see if I'd missed anything, I felt a tap on my left shoulder. I turned sideways in my seat to get a look at the dark-haired, tanned, green-eyed boy slouched in the seat behind me.

"Hey, I'm Collin," he said.

"Hey, I'm Lindsay," I said.

"What's up? Aren't you totally stoked to be in algebra?" he said.

"Yeah! Totally can't wait to multiply integers," I said, and we both laughed.

And that is how it started—nudging each other to whisper something funny, passing little notes back and forth about nothing. He made me laugh all the time, and I actually started looking forward to algebra, of all things. We even thought alike because we asked the same kinds of questions. We never saw each other outside of class, so at the end of the year I figured I probably wouldn't see him again until the next school year, and that was if we even had a class together. So I took a chance by asking him to give me a call over the summer—I never did that. I wasn't the type to just throw out a random, *Hey, K.I.T. 257-2530, call me! -Lindsay* But I did it even though I didn't think he would want to keep in touch because he knew I already had a boyfriend. It was a total shocker when I read what he wrote in my yearbook on the last day of school.

Lindsay,

Finally I got a hold of your yearbook. It's been awesome sitting next to you in Math.

You're a great looking and sweet girl and you should realize that because most girls aren't. Anyways it was funnier than hell when we joked around everyday. Call me sometime and we can subtract! JK! No, really I'd like to party with you or see you sometime or somewhere over this summer. So don't be afraid to call ok? See you around 347-8751

Later,

Love Collin Vance

I don't know the technical term for a swarm of butterflies, but that was what I had fluttering around my insides after reading those seven and a half sentences. They were pretty much all I could think about for the next few weeks of sunbathing with the Fab Four and evening BBQ's with the fam. I kept my feelings to myself, though, because I still hadn't worked up the nerve to call him or to break up with Bill Warner yet. I was living in this weird fluttery limbo, just savoring the *idea* of being with Collin—and then one day, it happened.

I was helping my mom in the garden. We were carrying river rocks from a pile in the driveway to the backyard. They were heavy, so we had to make a bunch of trips back and forth. On one of my trips back out to the front yard, I heard the phone ringing from inside the house, so I ran to answer it.

"Hello?" I said.

"Hey, Lindsay?" It was a male voice that I didn't recognize.

"Yeah?" I said. This didn't sound like the businesslike Bill Warner; this voice had a much more laidback vibe.

"It's me, Collin, from math class."

Holy crap!!! AAAAAAAHHHHH!!! It's him!!!!!

"Hey," I said, trying my best not to freak out.

"Hey. What's up?"

"Uh, I'm helping my mom in the garden," I said. *Really, Lindsay?!*

"Cool. Should I let you go?"

"No, no, it's fine. How are you?" I said and tried not to be a dork.

"Awesome, I just got back about an hour ago from visiting my mom's family for two weeks in Arizona and thought I'd call to see if you wanted to hang out."

"Yeah, totally! I'm free tomorrow. Do you want to go to the beach or something?" I said.

"Yeah, how about Santa Cruz?" he said.

"That would be awesome," I said. *Oh my God! I can't believe this is happening.*

"Sweet, I'll pick you up at two. I'm pretty wiped from the trip, so I'll be sleeping in for sure," he said.

"Okay, perfect. My address is Two-four-two Quay Lane in Redwood Shores," I said.

"Two-four-two Quay Lane. Got it," he said.

"See you tomorrow!" I said, trying to keep my voice steady.

"Later," he said.

"Later." I hung up the phone and did a happy dance. I could not believe this was happening. I had been wishing and hoping it would, but I never actually thought it would. I went through the rest of the day just floating. I couldn't sleep that night, I was so excited. I worried that we wouldn't have anything to talk about for a whole trip to the beach.

The next morning, I could barely eat anything with all of those butterflies swarming in my stomach. The clock dragged on; I could not wait for two o'clock to get here. I spent a solid two hours grooming myself, which was a good distraction, and it probably took me another hour just to pick out the perfect outfit. I chose my fluorescent pink bikini to compliment my tan and a white v-neck t-shirt and jean shorts to wear over it. I didn't want to look like I was trying too hard.

Close to two, I couldn't stand waiting anymore, so I went outside to wait for him. And then at approximately 2:03 p.m., I saw a VW bug driving toward my house. It was him. He pulled into my driveway, and my mouth must have dropped because he looked so good. His dark brown hair accentuated his golden skin. His green eyes sparkled as he smiled at me with his perfect white teeth. We got into his baby blue VW bug with its beefed-up engine and cruised to the beach with the sunroof open. My hair was flying in the wind, and I didn't even care, it felt amazing. I felt alive.

It turned out that we had so much to talk about; we had so much in common that we talked the whole time. When we finally made it over the hill and drove down the windy two-lane road that led to downtown Santa Cruz, we cruised up and down the main street for a while to find the perfect parking spot. We walked along the beach, talking the whole time, and then we sat and watched the sun set. That was our first date, and I knew I had to break up with Bill Warner.

I was surprised when Bill cried. I thought he would be excited at the prospect of being a free man in college. Maybe I'd bruised his ego and he was just upset that he hadn't thought of breaking up first with that big brain of his and all.

Despite that drama, I actually felt like my life was finally off the rollercoaster and on solid ground for the first time. I had the life that I thought I wanted. It was looking like it would be more exciting than I had ever imagined. The prospect of a cute new boyfriend was on the horizon. The only way to describe how I felt was a fluttery feeling in my chest at the thought of my senior year coming up and everything I wanted being within my grasp. The anticipation was such a distraction that I didn't see the destruction looming until it was too late to fix.

It was one year. One year that changed my life forever. The year that I went from seventeen to eighteen, the year that I finished being a child and started being an adult, at least on paper.

ten

_____

1989

After I broke up with Bill Warner, Collin and I went to the beach a lot and began seeing each other every day. He would wait for me out in the parking lot when I got off work at night to make sure I made it safely to my car. We would talk for a while, and when it was time for me to go home, he would take me in his arms and hug me with a tenderness that melted my heart and made me tingle inside. The nights grew colder as our senior year of high school approached.

One night near the end of summer, Collin turned to me and said, "Can I ask you something?"

"Um, yes."

"This may sound weird, but I have never felt this way about someone so fast. Will you be my girlfriend?"

Everything in my brain was telling me this was a bad idea, as we'd only known each other for a short time. I knew I should be cautious. I knew this is too soon. But even though I barely knew him, I felt like we knew each other on a different level, like from a past life or something.

I turned to look at him, with his piercing green eyes, tanned skin, and wide smile—how could I say no?

"You're right. It does sound weird, but yes," I said.

Collin and I were sad to see the summer disappear, but at the same time we were anxious to go back to school and surprise all of our friends with the news that we were officially boyfriend-girlfriend.

On the first day of school, I saw Lainey in the back corner of our homeroom class, and she waved me over. I made my way to the back of the classroom where she informed me that we had to sit in alphabetical order. Ugh! I hated that. I gave her a quick hug, then noticed my name on the seating chart a row over and three seats up. Okay, not too bad. We were still pretty close—close enough to exchange eyebrow raises and secret looks.

I'd been waiting for this all summer, but at eight o' clock in the morning, sitting at the hard wooden desk had a sobering effect on me. I went from feeling like Olivia Newton John as Sandra Dee in *Grease* to regular old Lindsay Trifling in high school. I found myself daydreaming about Collin constantly. I didn't even hear when the bell rang.

"Earth to Lindsay! Come in, Lindsay!" Lainey said, nudging me. "What is with you?"

"Oh my gosh, Lainey! I have a new boyfriend!" I grabbed my backpack and stood up.

"Oh my God! Who is he, and why have you been keeping this from me?" Lainey said, dragging me out of the classroom.

We made it out into the hallway, dodging everyone to get to our lockers.

"His name is Collin Vance, and I know, I should have told you sooner."

"I thought we were friends." Lainey crossed her arms, cocked her head to the side, and turned out her right foot, clearly annoyed that I had not shared this earth-shattering information with her.

"I know, I know, we are. It's just that, I mean, you were on vacation, and I had work, and I didn't want to tell anyone before I told you. But ahhhhh! Can you believe it?" I said.

"Oh my gosh! That is sooooo awesome! If you're into him," Lainey said.

"Wait, what do you mean 'if I'm into him'?"

"Well, it's just that he doesn't seem like your type, that's all. And I got sort of a weird vibe from him," she said, turning to face her locker to hide her furrowed brow.

"Not my type? Weird vibe?" I said, slamming my locker shut. "Explain yourself."

She turned back to look at me, eyebrows raised like she was about to tell me something I didn't want to hear. She knew me pretty well because I did not want to hear what she had to say if it was going to be negative, which I knew it would be.

There was nothing wrong with Collin. Okay, so his parents were divorced, but so were everyone else's. Lainey's parents were divorced! Talk about a weird vibe—her *mom* had moved out, not her dad, and he worked nights, leaving her alone to fend for herself. That was weird!

"I mean, I always pictured you with some Harvard guy wearing a polo shirt with a sweater tied over his shoulders. Collin just seems not like that, at all. He hangs out with Dan the pothead surfer, for crying out loud. It just seems like if you start hanging out with him, you won't want to hang out with us," she said.

Ugh! I couldn't believe she was saying this! "I did date the guy with the sweater, and it was a total snooze fest, remember Bill Warner? And there is noooo way I'm going to stop hanging out with you, Anna, and Jess."

Well, that was a lie, one of the many I would tell over the course of the year. Bill Warner had actually made me feel stupid because he read the newspaper and knew all kinds of current events. I spent all my time at school, practice, and doing homework; I didn't have time to read the newspaper. Collin never made me feel stupid; I actually felt smart for a change. Bill Warner was so serious all the time. Collin was the complete opposite of serious. He was always joking around and always had a huge smile on his face. Collin was all I could think about, and I was willing to do whatever it took to be with him.

"Okay, we'll just see about that," Lainey said. "See you at lunch?"

"Yeah, of course," I said, and we parted ways for second period.

eleven

As I was walking to our usual meeting spot on the parking lot steps, I bumped into Collin and his huge smile. His teeth looked unbelievably white compared to his smooth, unblemished, tan skin. He radiated an aura of laidback fun.

"Hey, me and Josh are cruisin' down to Taco Bell for a grub session. You in?" Collin said.

Oh my God, oh my God! Keep it together, stay cool, he just asked you to go to a fast-food restaurant. It's not like he asked you to the prom or anything.

"Um, yeah, sure, just let me let Lainey know not to wait for me." I twirled my hair to make it look like I really needed to mull the decision over.

"Cool, I'll walk with you."

Ahhh! He's walking with me, and we're at school.

"Cool." I saw Lainey up ahead. "Be right back." I jogged over to Lainey and gave her a hug.

"Let me guess, he asked you to go to lunch with him."

"Yes, I'm so excited."

"I don't want to say I told you so, but I told you so," she said, grabbing me by the shoulders to look me in the eye and furrowing her brow again, this time in mock seriousness. "Don't do anything I wouldn't do, or maybe don't do anything I would."

"I won't or I will, I promise!" I said, and Lainey and I started laughing.

Collin walked up to us.

"Have fun, you crazy kids!" Lainey said.

"Bye!" I said.

"I'm parked over here. We can take my V-Dub. Josh decided to go with Jake."

"Awesome!" I said.

We went to his car. Collin got in and leaned over to unlock the passenger door. I pulled open the door and sat in the front passenger seat.

I'd learned on our many trips to the beach over the summer that I had to slam the door to get it to close. It was a '66. He'd put a racing engine in it, so it was really loud when he started it up—a lot louder in the school parking lot than it had been on my street. He put the key in the ignition, started it up, and revved the engine.

"Yee-haw!" he said. I could feel the engine roar in my chest. "We need some tunes!" He popped in a cassette and started singing along to a Tesla song. I had never heard of this group before we started hanging out over the summer. He threw the car in reverse, screeched forward through the parking lot, came to an abrupt stop right before a speed bump, and drove over it super slowly like the car was made of glass, causing me to lurch forward.

"Oh, sorry, forgot to warn you. It's lowered, I have to go slow over the bumps in this parking lot so I don't scrape the front," Collin said.

"Um, it's okay," I said, trying to sound calm while my insides were flipping.

After about ten more "bumps," we arrived at Taco Bell, and I wanted to get out and kiss the ground.

We parked, and as we were walking in, Collin reached for my hand as if we always did this and hadn't just started being boyfriend and girlfriend. It seemed a little soon, but it sent shockwaves through my body, so I didn't resist. I wasn't used to someone being so bold and just doing whatever they felt like doing without worrying what anyone would think. It felt refreshing and exhilarating at the same time.

The line in Taco Bell was pretty long. We saw Josh and Jake at the front of the line, but they had already ordered.

"Duuuuude!" Collin yelled across the restaurant.

"Duuuuude!" Josh yelled back, "what took you so long?"

"The V-Dub, man!" Collin said.

By then, everyone was staring at us, and I was feeling a little self-conscious, but Collin didn't seem to notice or care what other people were doing.

The three of them started cracking up. I must have been standing there looking more bewildered than amused because the next thing I knew, Collin was putting his arm around me, pulling me in, and planting a kiss right on my forehead.

Whoa! I did not see that coming. I felt my face get hot, so I changed the subject.

"What do you normally get here?" I said. *Wow, that was lame. They only have, like, ten things on the menu.*

He laughed and said, "Good one!"

"Thanks," I said, trying to play it off like I had meant to be funny and not a dork.

We finally made it to the front of the line, but it was almost time to go back to school, so we got our food to go. He got the burrito supreme and four tacos. When the guy behind the counter handed him his bag, he lifted it up and said, "Grub sesh!" then leaned back and howled, "Hoo hoo!"

I laughed, grabbed the bag with my two tacos, lifted them up, and said, "Hoo hoo!"

Collin laughed, but the guy behind the counter was clearly annoyed with us because he yelled "Next!" which sent us into more laughter.

"Buzzkill! Let's go!" Collin said, and he took my hand again to lead me back out to the V-Dub.

A few more "bumps" later, we are back in the school parking lot with three minutes to spare. *I guess I'll be having my grub sesh in gourmet foods.*

He turned to look at me and smiled. I smiled back.

"Whoa, you have dimples in your cheeks when you smile," he said.

"Really?" I flipped down the visor to look in the mirror. "Huh, I never noticed that before."

He leaned over, turned my face toward him, and kissed me. He smelled a little like cigarettes and cinnamon. His skin was smooth and warm, and I forgot where I was until the bell rang and jolted me back to reality.

"Oh, crap! I gotta go. I can't be late again. I'm two tardies away from detention. Thanks for the ride."

"Hey, wait, did you want to meet up at the beach after school today? Some of my buds are going."

"Um, yeah, sure!" I yanked the door handle and had to lean my shoulder into the door to open it.

"Sweet! We'll meet you there at the regular spot. You can bring some friends," he said.

"Okay, cool." I slammed the door shut and ran to class.

twelve

The tardy bell rang just as I slid into my seat. My teacher started blabbing about the first day of school, blah, blah, blah. I turned back around to face her to make it seem like I was paying attention, but in reality, my brain was still stuck on my conversation with Collin.

This was so crazy. I had never gone to the beach on a school day. Lainey, Anna, and Jess would have to come with me. What was I going to tell my mom? She would never let me drive over the hill all the way to the beach by myself. I knew she would kill me. I knew she would ground me for the entire school year. I knew she would take away my car. I knew all of these things, but I was ready to start taking some chances and live life on the edge. I felt a heat come over my body, like I was on fire. This year was going to be great. I could feel it. Energy was coursing through me like I'd been plugged in. I was a physical phenomenon, electric charges forming an electrical current producing a magnetic field inside my body. Everything came flying at me, powerless to resist my pull. I couldn't even stop them, I could only contain them. I was the lion tamer, with my stool and whip. I wore the red vest and top hat. What was this circus that I had joined? I had joined it willingly. I was participating in the debauchery. I was no longer willing to stand on the sidelines and watch. It was my turn, and I was going to take it. I'd always let everyone else be the star. I was always in the shadows, the nice girl, the patient girl, the brunette, never the blonde who got to have all the fun. Well, not anymore. I was done with that. I was going to be the star of my life now.

My leg had fallen asleep from sitting. I heard the bell ring. I waited for everyone to leave before I stood up because I had to stomp my foot to get it to wake up—not exactly the "new star of my own life" image that I'd wanted to portray…

"And the academy award for wallflower-turns-prom-queen goes to Lindsay Trifling." The camera pans to me hunched over massaging my foot.

"Hang on one sec, I'll be right up."

The audience gasps.

"Oops, never mind. We thought you were a cool kid," the announcer says.

"No, wait, I am, really, wait," I say and hobble through the aisle, crawl up the steps, and stand on the stage adjusting my disheveled dress.

"Sorry, not this time, goodbye," the announcer's voice booms. The audience points at me in unison and breaks into hysterical laughter. A giant trapdoor opens up beneath me and swallows me up into the darkness.

"Lindsay, what are you doing? Let's go, the bell rang," Lainey said, peeking her head around the door.

"My foot fell asleep."

"Yeah, seems like your brain fell asleep." Lainey came in, hooked her arm through mine like we were about to square dance, and dragged me out of the room. "We can't be late for art on the first day. Mr. Jansen will be sad. We can totally be late tomorrow, though."

We both laughed. She was right. Art was our favorite class. Not only did we get to do art, but Mr. Jansen was one of the few cool teachers who totally "got" us.

"Lainey, hate to change the subject, but I need you to do me a huge favor," I said.

"Nothing good ever comes after that sentence," she said, giving me her annoyed look.

"No, it's not bad. It's good, kind of, but it will be fun. I promise," I said, holding up three fingers in a Girl Scout's honor gesture.

"What is it?"

"I need you, Anna, and Jess to come with me to the beach after school today." I squinted my eyes, bracing myself for her to yell at me.

"All the way to the beach?"

"Yeah," I said.

"Over the hill?" she said.

"Yeah."

"What's going on at the beach?"

"Collin Vance is going to be there with some of his friends."

"Collin Vance? Your new boyfriend?"

"Yes."

"Okay, I'll do it. On one condition—you explain to Mr. Jansen why we are late."

The tardy bell rang, and we ran to the closest table with a screeching of metal chair legs across linoleum and the thud of backpacks hitting the floor. The entire class looked in our direction.

"Well, so glad you could make it, ladies. Looks like I lost the bet," Mr. Jansen said, and the class laughed.

"Sorry, my foot fell asleep, and Lainey had to help me walk to class."

"Oh, of course, what else would keep you from getting to class on time?" he said, tilting his head and shrugging his shoulders before turning back toward the class. "As I was saying, this is advanced art, so I am expecting great things from you this year."

Mr. Jansen kept talking, and this time I was half-listening but still thinking about the beach after school. It was so unlike me to do something like this, and Collin Vance was so unlike Bill Warner. Bill never would have suggested anything like this, ever.

I glanced up at the clock and noticed that it was almost time for the bell to ring. I scribbled, *Meet me in the parking lot after school, tell Anna and Jess* on a piece of notebook paper and slid it to Lainey. She inched her hand over to accept the note as if we were conducting some major covert operation, peeked at it, and gave me a thumbs-up under the table.

The bell rang. Lainey gave me an exaggerated bear hug, tilting me side to side, and said, "How will I ever survive the next two periods without you?"

We both laughed.

"Bye, Lainey. See you in the parking lot after school," I said.

"Got it! Bye, Lindsay!" she said, walking backwards and blowing kisses.

"Lainey!" I yelled, as she was about to back into DJ Fatumalu'alu, the big-as-a-house starting lineman of the football team. "Oooh, too late!" I said, cringing.

Lainey laughed, turned, and ran down the hall. DJ hadn't even noticed.

Two classes and a stack of homework later, I sprinted to the parking lot to find my car. I didn't see Lainey yet, so I opened my trunk and flung my backpack in, muttering to myself about how lame it was that teachers gave homework on the first day.

Someone came from behind me and covered my eyes.

"Lainey, knock it off, you scared the bejeezes out of me, I almost cra—"

"It's not Lainey," a deep voice interrupted.

I peeled the hands from my eyes and turned to look at their owner.

My heart jumped into my throat—it was Collin. He laughed when he saw my expression.

I was feeling lightheaded and woozy, like someone had slipped something into my drink, only I hadn't had anything to drink.

"Hey, see you later," he said.

"Yeah, see you later," I think I said. I might have imagined it.

Collin turned and half-walked, half-jogged off to a small group of guys waiting at the other end of the parking lot.

thirteen

We were driving, just Lainey and I. Anna and Jess couldn't make it, or maybe they hadn't wanted to go, I hadn't gotten a straight answer out of Lainey, but it didn't make that much of a difference. I was going to go no matter what. The road curved left and right, left and right, left and right. Small hills made my stomach leap even though I was the one who was driving. The houses got farther and farther apart until there was only tall, dry grass and white fences lining the road. Lainey popped in the cassette—UB40. "Red Red Wine" started playing. Lainey bounced in her seat. We laughed. What other song would it be? Our friend Anna had made me this tape. She only listened to two songs—"Red Red Wine" and "Iko Iko." We came up to a dead end, only ocean ahead of us.

"Turn left," Lainey said.

"Are you sure?" I said.

"Yeeeeessss!" she said, exasperated.

"Okay, jeez." I made the turn and saw the sign for the beach on the right.

"There it is!" Lainey said, pointing at the sign.

I turned down the crunchy gravel road and parked next to Collin's VW bug. We jumped out before the dust settled. I grabbed my sweatshirt from the backseat and tied it around my waist. Lainey was still bouncing.

I bent down to get one last look at myself in the side mirror.

"You're gorgeous. Come on, let's go," she said and grabbed my hand.

"Lainey, wait! Do I have anything in my teeth?"

"Yeah, a big ol' green thingy right there in the middle. Just kidding, seriously, you look fine. Quit stalling. Let's go!" she said.

We headed toward the trail. It was steep and rocky. We made our way down, grasping onto branches sticking out of the cliff. Half-slipping and half-walking, we got to the bottom. The sand was rocky, so we kept our shoes on.

"Hey, over here!"

I looked up and saw Collin waving us over. I waved back. Lainey and I trudged through the sand toward the large firepit they were building.

"Ugh, this is a workout! Couldn't they have built this closer to the trail?" Lainey said.

"Yeah, feels like the Sahara except it's not hot and there is a giant ocean here," I said.

"Exactly!" she said.

We stopped to rest and were bent over laughing when Collin jogged over.

"What took you so long?" he said.

"Our girl here needed to finish primping," Lainey said, and I nudged her in the arm and smiled.

"Ouch!" she said.

"Cool. I wasn't sure you were coming or not. Come on over," he said.

We finished the journey to the firepit, and Collin introduced us to his friends.

"Hey, everyone, this is Lindsay and her friend. Lindsay and her friend, this is everyone," he said and laughed.

"Hi, Lindsay and her friend," they said in unison and laughed.

"Hi, everyone," I said.

"I'm just kidding. That's Dan, Josh, Jake, Todd, Darby, Jannay, and Derrick," Collin said, pointing each of them out.

I tried to connect each name to each face. I recognized Dan. He was in my gourmet foods class. I think he'd signed up for that class because he was stoned all the time and was just super hungry. I didn't really see him as the cooking type—he was a surfer, and that was it. Josh and Jake also went to our school, but I hadn't ever had any classes with them. They had matching mullets—business in the front, party in the back. The only difference between the two of them was that Josh had a lot of acne, and Jake had huge blue eyes that kind of popped out of his head. I didn't recognize Darby, Jannay, or Derrick. It turned out that they went to our rival school, Hillsdale High School, down the street. Darby was a petite girl with blonde hair that went past her butt. Jannay had dark brown hair like mine, but she had long bangs that she sprayed up into this huge hair arch over her forehead. Derrick looked like he had flunked out or had been held back for, like, five years or something, because he had a full mustache and beard.

"And I'm Lainey!" Lainey said, plopping down on the sand between Darby and Jannay. "Whatcha drinkin'?"

"Miller Lite, you want one?" Derrick said.

"Uh, no thanks. I'm not really a beer drinker, per se," Lainey said.

"I have a wine cooler if you want it," Darby said.

"Bartles and James! Sweet! I'll take it!" Lainey said, and I felt myself going into a trance, where you can still hear but your eyes freeze up. I became fixated on the flames flickering. They crackled, sending a trail of embers into the darkening sky.

What am I doing here? This is so unlike me. I'm not a rule breaker. My mom will literally kill me if she finds out I'm here. I've always done the right thing. I always let her know where I am. I always come home on time. Why am I having this burning urge to rebel? It feels wild. I feel wild. I'm out of control right now. I'm playing with fire. I'm drawn to the flame. I'm ready to jump into the fire.

I felt someone's hand on my shoulder, snapping me out of my trance.

"Hey," Collin said, "do you want to go sit over there?" He motioned to a cave-like overhang about fifty feet away.

"Okay, sure." I followed him across the rocky sand. It was starting to get cold, so I removed the sweatshirt from my waist, put it on, and sat next to him on a large log that appeared to be someone's abandoned firewood. I was readjusting my hair when I felt him looking at me.

"What?" I said, looking at him. *What is he thinking when he looks at me? Does he know that I am trembling inside? Does he know that I've never done anything like this before?*

"Nothing, it's just, I like you," he said.

"Oh, I like you, too." "Like" was a mild word for how I felt in that moment, but it would have been weird if I'd blurted out that just sitting next to him made my insides have goose bumps. I was kind of wishing I'd had one of those beers—maybe it would have calmed me down.

The wind whipped up.

"It's getting cold," I said, wrapping my arms around myself and shivering.

"Come here. I'll warm you up," he said.

I scooched over, and he put his arm around me.

"Better?"

"Yeah, thanks," I said, trying to keep my teeth from chattering and my heart from pounding. "So, how come I never saw you in algebra until the end of junior year?"

"I just transferred. My parents got divorced, and I moved in with my dad," he said.

"My parents are divorced, too, but that was a loooong time ago. My mom remarried, and I have a stepdad now."

"Cool."

"Yeah, I guess. I'm used to it now, but it was weird at first," I said, not wanting to discuss why my mom had gotten divorced and how she and I had basically been roommates from when I was four until we'd moved in with my stepdad two years before, and, presto, we'd become an instant family.

"Hey, look at the love birds!" Lainey yelled, stumbling toward us.

"Oh boy, here she comes," I said, removing Collin's arm from around my shoulders and standing up.

"I think it's time to go." I looked at my watch, and it was almost six o'clock. Crap! My mom would be so pissed if I wasn't home by 6:30, and I still had to take Lainey home.

"Go? You just got here," he said.

"Yeah, I know, sorry. I told Lainey I would get her home before it got dark," I said instead of telling him how lame I really was for having to be home before dinner.

"Okay, I'll walk up with you."

"Thanks," I said.

Lainey picked me up and swung me around.

"I love this girl!" she said, then dropped me and fell over.

"Love you, too! Okay, let's go." I helped her up, and we made our way back to the bonfire to say goodbye. I couldn't really remember everyone's name, so I just went with the generic, "Bye, everyone!"

"Bye," they said.

"Collin, you're leaving, too? Dude, you're my ride," Josh said.

"No, dude, I'm just walking them up. Chill," Collin said, and he flipped his dark wavy hair back, reminding me of Keanu Reeves in a *Bill and Ted's* kind of way, except cooler.

As we made our way back up the steep path, I started to wonder what Collin was thinking. I mean, I felt kind of bad that we couldn't stay longer, but my mom would have probably killed me if I'd waltzed home after dinner without letting her know where I was.

I wondered if Collin's parents were okay with all of this. I knew they were divorced and everything, but it kind of seemed like he did this sort of thing all the time.

We finally reached the top.

"Hey, you parked right next to me, cool!" Collin said.

"Oh, yeah," I said.

He reached for my hand.

"Here, Lainey," I threw her the keys. "I'll be right there."

"What?" she said, and I heard the giant ball of key chains where I kept my house and car keys drop to the ground. "Oh, okay, got it, wink, wink."

I turned away while she was fumbling for the keys, and Collin snatched me up and planted a solid kiss on my lips that set a tingle over my entire body. Whoa! I was not expecting that, but I went with it. He stopped to look me in the eye, and then we both went back in for another kiss—longer this time and with tongue. I was leaned up against the VW, and he was pressing his weight on to me. I couldn't believe this was happening.

I had kissed before, but this was different than any kiss I'd ever had. I mean, the list of boys I had kissed was actually pretty long, starting with Justin Seifert in fifth grade and followed by Jake Kwan in sixth grade, though both those kisses had pretty much been pecks on the lips, no tongue or anything, you almost couldn't even call them kisses, actually. Those had been followed by a pretty long dry spell in middle school until Ramone Ruelas in my freshman year of high school. You would have thought that with a name like *RRRRamone RRRRuelas*, the kissing would have been hot and heavy, but it had actually been more of a tutorial. He'd given me pointers on how to French kiss since I had never done it before, and that kind of took the passion right out. But he'd been a year older than me, and I'd just been grateful that someone even liked me enough to teach me how to kiss.

After that, aided by the fact that I got my braces off and wasn't a complete dork anymore, I practically went on a kissing spree. The boy from the bus stop, the boy from Taco Bell, the boy from across the street, the boy from English class...but none of them were like this. Well, of course, there was Bill Warner my junior year. He wasn't a bad kisser, it was just more comfortable, like an old married couple. But with Collin, kissing became something else entirely.

I had to push him back to catch my breath. He pushed back. All of a sudden, I felt self-conscious. I couldn't believe I was doing this. My arms were around his neck, his arms were around my waist; I pushed him back again, placing my hands on his shoulders and locking out my arms.

"I can't, I have to, I gotta go," I said.

"Just one more," he said.

"Okay," I gave in.

Honnnnnnnnnnnnnnk! Lainey laid on the horn. My heart stopped and started again!

"Holy shit! What the hell?" Collin said.

"I gotta go. See you tomorrow." I pushed him back again and turned to my car.

He grabbed my arm again before I could get in and stole another kiss. "Promise?"

"I promise," I said, then got in my car and shut the door. Lainey had already turned my car on to listen to the radio. Collin stood and watched me throw it in reverse. I waved, and he waved back. The dust swallowed him up, and we got back on the main street.

"Well, that was entertaining!" Lainey said.

"Sorry. I don't know what came over me."

"Yeah, it was like watching a Madonna video." Lainey wrapped her arms around herself, closed her eyes, and started air-kissing.

"Oh my God! Was it that bad?"

"Kind of, but I totally would have done the same if it had been Darren Yanaguchi." she said.

The cassette flipped over and started playing "Iko Iko." Lainey cranked up the volume, danced in her seat, and drummed out the beat on the dashboard. My mind kept playing that kiss over and over again like a cassette tape in my head. It had been so intense, like flames, and I couldn't pull away. It all seemed like too much, but I still had this urge to go straight into the fire. My brain was telling me to just walk away, not to see him again, but my body wasn't listening.

I pulled up in front of Lainey's house. She got out, hoisted her backpack over her shoulder, and said, "Bye, see you tomorrow."

"Wait, Lainey!" I leaned forward to make eye contact with her through the open car door. "Thank you for going with me, and don't say anything."

"You're welcome. It was fun, and don't worry, your secret is safe with me." Lainey pantomimed locking her mouth and throwing away the key, then slammed the door shut and waved. I waved back with a weak smile, thinking, *How I am going to explain my tardiness to my mother?*

fourteen

By the time I pulled up in front of my house, it was 7:05 p.m. *Okay, I'm only thirty-five minutes late. I think I can pull this off.* I walked through the front gate and through the little courtyard to our front door. I put my key in the lock, hesitating for a second. I had to get a story together. Once I figured it out, I turned the doorknob, took a deep breath, and opened the door. I could see my mom standing in the kitchen tossing a salad in an enormous salad bowl. She turned at the sound of me closing the door.

"Ugh, finally! Where have you been?" my mom said, salad tongs still in hand.

"Hi, sorry. I had practice, and then as I was leaving Lainey asked for a ride home."

"I thought you said you didn't have practice today. And why didn't Lainey take her car?" she said, placing down the salad tongs and putting her hands on her hips.

"Um, yeah, that's what I thought, but I was wrong. And Lainey did have her car, but she lost her car keys, so I drove her home to go get them." I said. *Oh God, this story is getting worse by the minute.*

"Hmmm, well, I wish you would have called. My salad is wilted now," she said, throwing her arms up and letting them slap down to her thighs.

"I know, I'm so sorry. I just thought that if I stopped to make a call, it would take even longer." *Deep breath, deep breath, keep it together, she's buying it.*

"Okay, but next time you need to call if you're going to be late," she said, turning back to her salad. "Chiiiiiiip! Dinner's ready."

Thank God, she'd moved on. I ran upstairs to change before she detected any campfire smell remnants. *Quick, find something else to wear.* I flung off my sweatshirt and blouse and threw on the first sweatshirt I saw in the clean pile of laundry sitting on my desk chair. I pulled down my jeans, hopping on one foot to free the first leg and then the next leg.

"Liiiiiiiiiiiiindsay!" I heard my mom yell.

"Coming!" I yelled. I dug through the pile to find some bottoms. I found some that totally didn't match, but I didn't have time to mess around. I pulled my hair back into a high bun and ran back downstairs and through the living room and slid into my seat at the dining room table.

"Mmmm, big salad, my favorite," I said. "Big Salad" is usually what we had at the end of the week when my mom was trying to use up leftovers. She chopped up all of the random ingredients and threw them together with lettuce. I ate as fast as I could so I could avoid any more questions. My mom and stepdad started talking about something that had happened at work. I zoned out and thought about Collin and our kiss. What was I going to say to him tomorrow? How was I going to be able to concentrate on anything when all I could do was think about him? Maybe I should write him a note and let him know how I felt? No, that would be crazy. I felt crazy. Maybe I just needed to go up and do homework, that might help me think about something else. I needed to get out of here now.

"Thanks for dinner. I've got homework," I said, pushing out my chair and interrupting their conversation.

"Already, on the first day?" my mom said.

"Yeah, can you believe that? Senior year teachers are harsh," I said, but really I was thankful to be able to lock myself in my room. I made my way up the stairs. My room was the first door on the right. I went in and closed the door behind me. I grabbed my summer reading book that I was supposed to have finished over the summer so I could skim it in order to write a five-paragraph essay about it in class tomorrow. *Wuthering Heights*—here we go, Catherine and Heathcliff. *Wait, what is happening here? Is*

Heathcliff her brother? Is she a ghost? There's more than one Catherine. I was confused. I threw the book down; I couldn't focus. All I could think about was Collin. I decided to write him a note.

Collin,

Hey, how's it goin'? I had fun at the beach. Thanks for inviting me. I hope we can hang out again soon. I have cheerleading practice tomorrow and Friday after school but maybe we can get together on Saturday or something. I think Lainey might be having a back to school party at her house. I'll keep you posted.

Write Back.

Later,

Lindsay

Oh my God! I couldn't give this to him. I needed to talk to Lainey first. Ugh! It was fine, I'd just give him the stupid note. He already knew I liked him, he'd asked me to be his girlfriend.

I folded the note in half the long way and then again until it was a long skinny rectangle, and then I folded up the corner, making a triangle. I kept folding it over, making more triangles until it became one small origami-style triangle, and then I tucked in the end. I wrote Collin's name on the outside and resisted the urge to draw little hearts all over it. That would definitely be over the top.

I dropped the note into the front pocket of my backpack and reached for *Wuthering Heights* again. I pulled my English notebook, my dictionary/thesaurus, and my highlighter from my backpack and spread them out on the beige carpet of my bedroom floor. I tucked my knees up to my chest and leaned against my bed to start reading.

My eyelids felt heavy. I felt my head nod, and I jerked it back up to try to stay awake, but then I gave in to sleep. I had the most bizarre dream. I was back at the beach, only this time instead of jeans and a sweatshirt, I was wearing a large sunbonnet with a ribbon tied under my chin and a giant dress with petticoats and a corset. I was standing by the water's edge, and Collin was there wearing a tweed jacket, a bowtie, and heavy wool pants. He was holding my hand. He leaned in to kiss me, but my bonnet got in the way, so I untied it and flung it into the ocean. Lainey and Dan were there, too, rowing an outrigger canoe. Lainey caught my bonnet and put it on and waved at us. Collin pulled me in for an embrace, and we both fell to the sand. He was lying on top of me now. His scent was something I couldn't place, smoky but clean, like a campfire and laundry detergent. We looked at each other for a moment then closed our eyes, and our lips meet. We were kissing, and the water was lapping toward us; each wave felt colder than the last. We rolled to the side, still kissing, and I felt something sharp on my cheek in the sand. Was it a rock? A twig?

I woke up to find that I had fallen asleep on the floor with my cheek resting on the edge of the book. Whoa, that was weird. I pushed myself up off the floor, climbed onto my unmade bed, pulled the covers up, and tucked them under my chin, hoping to keep the dream going. But it was over. I couldn't get it back.

I drifted off to dreamless sleep only to be awoken what seemed like five seconds later to Michael Jackson blaring from my clock radio telling me to "Beat it!" I reached over and hit the snooze button. I was not ready for this day. My obsession with Collin had taken over my brain. I was probably going to bomb that essay, but more importantly—what was I going to wear today? I needed to figure out something that looked put together but not like I was trying too hard. Ugh! After a shower and about six wardrobe changes, I decided to go with my black mini skirt, white t-shirt, jean jacket, and medium-size gold hoops to complete the look. I felt better. I ran downstairs into the kitchen to grab a banana and head out the door.

"Bye!" I yelled to no one in particular.

fifteen

Tuesday

After school, I headed to my locker to grab my gym bag so I could change into my practice clothes. I had my backpack on the ground and was bent over trying to shove my ten-pound physics book into it when I felt someone poke their finger into my side. I jumped up and screamed.

"Whoa! Sorry!" Collin said.

"You scared the crap out of me!"

"I'm sorry, give me a hug," he said with his arms outstretched.

"Okay, but don't do that again." I hugged him.

"Okay, I won't," he said and nuzzled his face into the side of my neck, turning my legs into rubber. "Do you want to come over to my house tomorrow? My dad is out of town," he said.

I did want to go with him, but since school had started I'd had so much homework, and with practice every day, I hardly had any extra time. Collin was really understanding about this since we'd been having lunch together for practically a whole month by then. I couldn't believe it was already October.

"Um, yeah, maybe, I have to check, and I'll let you know. I have practice, but maybe I can leave early."

"Cool. See you tomorrow." He walked backward and waved.

"See you tomorrow." I slammed my locker shut and hoisted my backpack and gym bag together over my shoulder.

Wednesday

I was sitting in my fourth period Art in our Lives class, which was basically an art history class. You would think that after taking art for three straight years I would have placed out of this class, but no, there I was learning about why Rubin had decided to paint round women. I decided that I should write Collin a note to let him know that I wouldn't be able to go to his house today. I had forgotten I had a hair appointment, and my government and physics teachers were conspiring to ruin my life with all of this homework. I ripped a page out of my notebook and wrote:

Collin,

Art N R Lives is so boring, so I thought I should do something to keep me awake. I had fun going to lunch with you yesterday. Someone gave Lainey a piece of Lemon pie, isn't that neat. I don't know if you helped make it or not but if you did, Lainey's gonna eat it. Gosh, I must be really bored if I keep talking about lemon pie. I don't think I can go to your dad's house with you tonight because I have to do 5 current events for Amer. Gov't and I have to study for a physics test, and I might be getting a perm after practice. Maybe we can hang out this weekend. The bell just rang, gotta go.

XO,

Lindsay

I folded up the note and ran out of class.

Friday

Lindsay,

So how's it going dimples? I'm sitting in Gourmet Foods bored off my ass. I didn't make the lemon pie but that sounds screamin' good. We have a substitute and we are watching a video. Darren and Dan are about to get high on the balcony. I don't feel like getting high for a while.

Anyways, enough of that. How's it going for you lately? Haven't talked to you in a while. I've gotten a lot of things accomplished for me lately. I drove my car down to the shop so it's getting fixed next week. Wow, isn't this letter totally fucking exciting!!! By the way, I think your perm looks hella awesome on you. I can't believe how fast this year is going by. Everyday just flies by for me. We can hang out on Saturday. I'll pick you up since the VW will be out of the shop. Well I can't think of anything to talk about except I think you are awesome and I'll see you at lunch.

XO,

Collin

sixteen

Saturday

I'd driven through Hillsborough, California, before. It was all windy roads, sharp uphill turns, and mega mansions interspersed between regular-sized homes and tall trees. I'd always wondered what it would be like to live in one of these houses.

We turned off the main road up a steep driveway. The house revealed itself as we reached the crest. A large, postmodern, split-level home stood alone on the flat part of the lot. It was surrounded by trees, and no neighboring homes were in sight. It felt a million miles away from my own neighborhood, which was jam packed with tall and skinny homes, parked cars, and kids riding their bikes down the middles of the streets. This home looked empty, lifeless, and drab, with its sharp edges painted a dull greenish gray. A feeling of sadness washed over me that I couldn't explain.

"Oh, shit, my dad's home," Collin said, and I noticed the open garage to the left side of the house where a dark green Jaguar was parked.

"Is that bad? It would be nice to meet him," I said.

"There's nothing nice about Edward J. Vance, III, president of Golden State Bank. He's probably pissed at me for not putting my dishes in the dishwasher, and I'm pretty sure I didn't take out the trash either," he said, turning off the engine. "I'm just gonna run in and grab a jacket, and then we can go hang somewhere else."

"Are you sure you don't want me to meet him?" I said.

"Ah, what the hell. He probably won't be as mad if you're with me. Let's go."

We got out of the car and walked through the garage. It was empty apart from the car—not a bike or a tool to be found. Collin opened the door to the house, which led to a staircase covered in dark gray slate tiles. At the top of the stairs there was a large entryway to the right with more slate tiles and a family room to the left with dark brown wood floors and paneling that opened to a kitchen with dark brown cabinets. The family room had a brown-and-gray plaid sofa and a leather club chair. The only light filtering into the room was from a bare sliding glass door, and through it, I could see an empty patio surrounded by trees. There were no pictures on the walls or decorations of any kind. Through the far side of the entryway, there looked to be a formal living and dining room.

A voice came booming from that direction. "Get your ass in here!"

"Dad, I have a friend with me," Collin yelled back, and we walked toward the living room.

Edward J. Vance, III, was sitting on the lone sofa in an enormous room with vaulted ceilings. This room was in stark contrast with the rest of the home. It jutted out of the front of the house like a giant fishbowl. There was a stone fireplace at the opposite end of the room flanked by floor-to-ceiling windows.

Mr. Vance removed his glasses and set them on the coffee table, the only other piece of furniture in the room. He turned to look at us and stood, revealing his tall, lanky frame. He had the same body type as Collin but looked almost as hardened as the slate floors. Collin was right—he was definitely an Edward, not an Ed or Eddie. Even in his weekend non-work clothes, he looked uncomfortable.

"Hello," he said and reached his hand out to shake mine.

"Dad, this is Lindsay," Collin said.

"Hello, Mr. Vance, it's nice to meet you," I said, returning his handshake and feeling like I had just taken a time machine back to the sixties. He nodded at me and then turned his attention to Collin.

"Collin, I thought we had agreed that you were not to go out until all of the chores had been done."

"Come on, Dad, it's Saturday."

"I don't care what day it is, we had an agreement," Mr. Vance raised his voice.

I looked down at my feet and took a step back to avoid the awkwardness.

"I told you I would do it later," Collin said.

"You must think I'm an idiot. I mean, I would have to remove half of my brain to be able to think like you!" Mr. Vance threw his arms up.

I took another step back. The conversation had gone from zero to a hundred in ten seconds. This had definitely been a bad idea. Collin's face was beet red.

Suddenly, fists were flying, and it was a brawl with grunting, heavy breathing, and heavy bodies. I felt their weight even though they were not touching me. I backed up to a window, wishing I could morph through it and disappear into the trees. I noticed there was one decoration in the corner, a vase on a stand. They knocked into it. It shattered on the floor. Mr. Vance's hand was cut. He shoved Collin back.

"Get the hell out!" he yelled at Collin.

Collin got to his feet, grabbed my hand, and pulled me back through the slate entryway and down the stairs. We got in his car. He revved the engine. He drove too fast down the driveway. I was trembling. I had my eyes closed. We drove. We didn't talk. I started praying, and then I had a sudden flashback.

I was nine years old, and I was sitting in the front seat of the orange Ford pick-up truck my dad drove for work. He'd come to pick me up to stay at his house for the weekend. It seemed like a long drive from my mom's house in Grass Valley to my dad's house in Marysville. There was only one way to get there, a windy two-lane highway I hated driving on because my dad drove too fast, and when someone didn't go fast enough in front of him, he would drive on the other side of the highway to pass them. My parents never took me to church, but I had friends who went, so I knew about God, and the fact that they didn't take me to church wasn't going to stop me from talking to God in my head during times like this. *Dear God,* I said to myself, *please don't let my dad kill us, thank you.*

By the time we reached the small yellow house with perfectly manicured grass that we weren't allowed to play on, it was starting to get dark.

"My head really hurts," I finally got the courage to say once we were inside the house, and the tears began to flow.

"Then quit your crying and go to bed! What am I supposed to do about it?" my dad snapped.

I couldn't stay in that room with him one more second. I went into my half-brother Caleb's room, took off my shoes, and climbed up the chunky wooden bunk bed to the top bunk. My head was throbbing as I put it on the pillow, and I cried until I fell asleep.

Back in the present, I finally understood Collin. I got why he did whatever he wanted. He was trying to escape from his father, just like I'd wanted to do when I was nine.

When the car came to a stop and I heard the engine cut off, I opened my eyes. We were at the beach. I looked at Collin. His face was wet with tears, and he had his arms straight out with his hands hanging over the steering wheel.

"I'm sorry," I said, not exactly sure why I felt the need to apologize, but it felt like the right thing to do.

"Thanks," he said, wiping his face with the heel of his hand. He turned toward me and gave me a hug. We stayed in this embrace for what seemed like twenty minutes. My arm felt like it was falling asleep, so I pulled back from him.

"My dad's an asshole," he said.

"Yeah, mine, too," I said, and we both laughed.

"Screw them!" he said.

"Yeah, screw them!" I said.

"Hey, do you want to walk down to the beach?"

"Yeah," I said, and we got out of the car.

Collin grabbed a towel from the backseat, and we headed down the steep trail to the beach. He held my hand to help keep me from slipping. When we reached the bottom of the trail, we keep walking, trudging through the rocky sand until we got to the cave-like overhang where we'd sat the last time we'd been here together. There was not another person on the beach even though it was a Saturday at noon. It was October 7th, so the temperature was in the mid-sixties, but the beach felt cold with the ocean breeze coming in. It felt more like the temperature was in the fifties.

"Hey, it's our spot," Collin said, and laid the towel down on the sand in front of a large piece of driftwood. He knelt down on the towel and patted his hand beside him, my cue to sit down next to him. When I knelt down and sat next to him, he put his arm around me, and we leaned back on the driftwood.

"So, why is your dad an asshole?" Collin asked.

"I don't really like to talk about it, but he used to yell a lot," I said. I had a flashback to this one time when I was about nine years old, and I had just come in for lunch after being outside with my little brother all morning. My dad didn't let us come in and out of the house if the air conditioner was on, and if the air conditioner wasn't on, he wouldn't let us in because it would let in flies. If we were out, we had to stay out, and if we were in, we had to stay in. But if we stayed in, he would yell at us for being noisy, so we always stayed out.

Anyway, the shades to the sliding glass door were normally open, but this one time I had to open the blinds in order to get to the sliding glass door. They were kind of heavy for me, so they were a little crooked. I didn't have the skill or the strength to get them straight. When my dad saw this, he flipped out, went right to the shades, and while he straightened them, he shouted, "Jesus Christ, we don't live in Olivehurst!"

Olivehurst was a nearby town that was mostly made up of trailer parks and junkyards, and my dad thought everyone who lived there was a lowlife. For some reason, this made me laugh, and that was the kiss of death. My dad sent me to my room—well, it was really Caleb's room—for the rest of the day with no lunch or dinner. I wasn't sure what he was hoping to accomplish by that, but it just made me hate him even more. He was the lowlife, and I couldn't wait to get out of that house.

"*Used* to yell at you?" Collin asked me. "You mean, he doesn't anymore?"

"I guess he still does, I just don't see him much anymore since my mom and I moved, and she married my stepdad." I really didn't want to talk about this stuff, so I changed the subject. "So where does your mom live?"

"She lives in Foster City with my brother, Christopher. I was living with her, but her place is kind of small, and I was tired of sharing a room. Christopher is a total dork, just sits around on his lazy ass playing Nintendo all day." Collin reached for my hand. "Thanks for being with me today. You're so awesome." He looked me straight in the eye.

"Thanks, I think you're so awesome."

Before I could say another word, he leaned in, and I could smell that laundry detergent smell from my dream. It was cold, but I felt a heat radiating off of him as he pulled me in for a kiss. It started off slow and tender at first, just his full lips on mine. He eased me down so we were lying on the towel on the sand next to each other, and then he went in for the deep kiss with tongue. He was more forceful now. It was exciting and uncomfortable at the same time. This was not really the way I had envisioned this moment, but I couldn't seem to break away from him. I couldn't say no. It was like he had cast some sort of spell over me, and I was in a trance. I let him take over my body. I completely surrendered, and then it was over. He whispered, "I love you" in my ear.

I was kind of in shock about what had just happened. How could I have gotten so wrapped up in my emotions that I'd just thrown all common sense out of the window? This wasn't my first time, but still. I'd lost my virginity to Bill Warner last year after my seventeenth birthday. It had been a completely planned event. Bill had wanted everything to be just right, and we'd talked about it for weeks. He'd even discussed with me that it might not actually feel that great the first time. He talked the entire time. I think Bill Warner and Raoul Ruelas worked from the same, *How to Teach a Babe to do Stuff* handbook because the experience felt like a tutorial. He had been right, though, the first time had been awkward and uncomfortable, to say the least. Even though Bill, being the honor student that he was, always used protection, I'd decided to put myself on the pill just in case. I was thanking my lucky stars that I'd gone on the pill because this was probably the craziest, most irrational thing I had ever done.

seventeen

Monday Morning

Collin,

That was an intense "date". I think you're so awesome and I'm so happy you asked me to be your girlfriend. I didn't think you liked me that much and that maybe you liked someone else more. Anyway, you make me smile and feel all tingly inside. I can't believe I'm telling you this mushy stuff. Hopefully we can hang out next weekend too. Maybe you can come over to Lainey's with me. I think her dad will be out of town and she's going to have a little soiree (aka PARTY!!!). Anyway, I think you're awesome, did I say that already? Oh well, it's true! Gotta go, write back.

XO,

Lindsay

Monday Afternoon

Lindsay,

Well here I am writing you another note. I just wanted to tell you that I Love You!!! You are a very sweet girlfriend to me and I hope our relationship only gets better than it already is. Don't ever think that I would "like" someone more than you because no Fifi compares to my Lindsay. Anyways, enough of my mushy truth. You see, you even get me to write this to you. I can't wait to go out with you this weekend. I also can't wait to drive my bug. Wow, awesome. "Hey, this is U.S. History I see a globe right there!" I'll bet your laughing right now. Smile and be happy for the day. I'll see you when I see you.

Later

I Love You,

Collin

"Lainey, you are never gonna believe what happened this weekend!"

"Lemme guess, you and Collin ran off and got married!" Lainey said.

"Ha, ha, very funny. No, but we are definitely, officially boyfriend and girlfriend, if you know what I mean! Ahhhhh!" I yelled and grabbed onto Lainey's arms, jumping up and down.

"No way! I was totally kidding, but oh my God! I'm so happy for you! Ahhhhh!" she yelled and jumped up and down, too. "So are you guys coming to my house this weekend?"

"I think so, I sent Collin a note to ask him if he wants to go," I said.

"Awesome! It's gonna be hella fun! My sister will be home from LA and is going to buy us some adult beverages. I am totally stoked!"

"Me, too! I can't wait! I gotta go, I'm late for practice. I'll call you later! Bye!"

"Bye!" Lainey dipped me one last time before she let me go.

Wednesday Night

Practice that week had been uneventful. We had a home game the following week, so we had to dance to the band music, which wouldn't have been that bad if the band was good. But it wasn't, and they played everything super slowly, so it felt like we were dancing in slow motion.

That night I wanted to get home and eat dinner quickly so I could call Collin to make sure he got my note and find out if he wanted to go to Lainey's party. I scarfed down my dinner and escaped to my room. I put my radio on to help muffle the sound, as I didn't need anyone listening to my conversation. I dug Collin's number out of my backpack, picked up the phone, and dialed.

One ring...two rings...three rings—Crap, is he not home?—Four rings—oh my God, I should just hang up—

"Hello?" Collin answered. I froze, unable to speak. "Dude, is anyone there?" he said again.

"Hey, it's me," I croaked out.

"Lindsay?" he said.

"Yeah, hey."

"Hey, what's up?"

"Did you read my note?" I said.

"Yeah, it was awesome."

"Thanks. Do you want to go with me to Lainey's party?"

"Yeah, I was going to call you later."

"Really?" I said.

"Yeah. I don't think I'm up for a big party with Lainey's crew. I thought maybe you might want to come over to my mom's house. She lives in a condo complex that has a hot tub," he said.

"Um, yeah, that sounds fun, but I kind of told Lainey I would go to her party. Maybe we could just stop by and then do the hot tub thing."

"Yeah, that's cool."

"Awesome, I'll meet you at your mom's, and we can drive over together," I said.

"I'll give you her address tomorrow."

"Cool."

"Hey, Collin, can I ask you something?"

"Yeah."

"I thought you didn't like going to your mom's. How come you want to go there?"

"Well, remember Saturday? I'm not exactly welcome in my dad's house anymore," he said.

"Oh, yeah. I guess that makes sense."

"My mom let me convert the garage into a room, so I don't have to stay with Chunkie—I mean Christopher." He laughed. "Plus, this way I get to see your screamin' body in a bikini."

I hoped he couldn't feel my blush through the phone because my face was about a thousand degrees.

"You think my body is screamin'?"

"Hell, yes!"

"Thanks! I think you're screamin', too." *Oh my God, did I just say that?*

"We can put our screamin' bodies together," he said.

"And we can kiss all weekend," I said, then heard a knock at my door. "Oh shit! I gotta go. My mom's knocking. I'll write you a note. Bye," I whispered, then hung up.

"Hey, come in," I said to my mom.

"Hi, I made you some dessert," my mom said, peeking her head around the door. "It's strawberries with whipped cream. Were you on the phone just now?"

"Um, oh yeah, I was just calling someone about an assignment. Wow, that looks really good. Thank you!" I said, taking the bowl from my mom. "Well, gotta get back to work." I really did not want to get into a whole big discussion with her.

"Okay, don't stay up too late," my mom said.

"Okay, I won't. Thanks again!"

Oh my God, did I almost just have phone sex and have my mom interrupt? This was crazy. I couldn't believe I was feeling like this over a boy. I couldn't believe I was making stuff up to my mom. This was so unlike me. I didn't do stuff like this. I didn't tell lies. I didn't sneak around. I didn't have these urges to run off and have sex in public. It was like my brain turned off when I was with Collin, and I went all animalistic.

I picked up my ten-pound physics book, plunked it down in front of me, and opened it, hoping it would shed some light. *Chapter 3, Inertia. Newton's first law of motion: an object in motion stays in motion.*

Well, that explained it all right. Collin and I were definitely in motion.

Thursday

Lindsay,

Hey gorgeous! What's up? Interesting phone conversation last night. I don't really know what to say. I wonder what your note will say. I can't believe it's already Thursday. By the way, if my handwriting sucks, it's because I'm writing this on Dan's bed. It probably blew out a gust of smoke too. I'm stoked, I get my car on the road tomorrow. "Hey, and your invited too" as Spicoli says. Anyways, this letter hasn't gotten mushy enough yet so here I go: I love you and I hope were together forever! Wow! Totally Awesome! Smile Lindsay as I say in every note. I hope we kiss all weekend too.

Later

Love Ya, Collin

Collin,

I hope you didn't think I was being too aggressive on the phone. It's just that I really like you, love you actually and have a tendency to loose my mind when I'm talking to you. You make me a little crazy but I love it! I can't wait too see you this weekend. What's your mom's address?

Love,

Lindsay

Lindsay,

First of all, you could never be too aggressive are you kidding me? You're screamin'! Second of all, my mom's address is 707 Marina Vista Dr., Fosler City, just off of Hillsdale Blvd. in the Edgewater complex. After you go in the gate turn right. I'll be waiting for you Saturday at 7pm sharp! Third of all, I can't wait to see you either so smile!

Later,

Love, Collin

eighteen

Saturday

I pulled into the Edgewater condo complex and turned to the right. I saw Collin sitting on the curb smoking. I pulled into the empty parking spot next to him. He took one last drag from the cigarette, dropped it on the ground, and crushed it out with his foot. I hadn't been sure if he smoked or not, but he had smelled like smoke the last time we'd been together.

I got out of my used, metallic brown Honda Prelude and shut the door. My mom and stepdad had bought it for me when I turned seventeen-and-a-half, partly because they'd felt bad for forgetting my birthday for six months, and partly because they'd been tired of me borrowing their cars all the time.

"I didn't know you smoked," I said.

"Yeah, I'm trying to quit. Does it bother you?" he said.

I had a flashback to when I was thirteen, when my dad was with his third wife, whom I hated. He'd cheated on Meg, my first stepmom, with her. I remembered looking at my dad's third wife as she applied thick black lines around her entire eyes, intensifying the beadiness of them. Wasn't eyeliner supposed to make your eyes look bigger? She was smoking a cigarette; the air in the room was stagnate, and smoke hung over the ashtray. She finished lining her eyes and waited for her curling iron to heat up. She took a drag of her cigarette. She tried to make small talk with me in her raspy smoker's voice.

"It's supposed to be ninety-five degrees today and—" she was interrupted by a hacking cough, and then continued, "—humid."

"Great," I said, only half listening, more focused on the smoke curling out of her mouth as she spoke. *What kind of life is this?* I wondered. Day after day, sitting around and smoking, sitting at the kitchen counter, putting on make-up—for what? She wasn't going anywhere or doing anything except barking orders at children. I was sure she hadn't planned on having to look after three extra kids in addition to her own two. I was sure that didn't cross a person's mind when they hooked up with strange men at bowling alleys. Maybe if she'd asked my dad a few questions— *Are you married? Do you have kids? Are you an abusive jerk?*—she would have saved herself a lot of headaches. But there we were, staring at each other.

Finally, she gave me a chore—she probably sensed my silent judgment.

"The toilet brush and spray are under my sink. My toilet needs to be cleaned today before your dad comes home for lunch. Oh, and make sure you really get under the rim this time," she said with a straight face.

Seriously, had she not seen Cinderella? She and my dad could have had their own show...*How Not to Parent*. I was actually relieved, though, and kind of happy to scrub a toilet instead of having to sit there for one more minute. I definitely did not want to catch the wrath of my dad—God forbid the toilets were not scrubbed. I was so over the whole situation. It was just weird. The house my dad bought had been an old rescue mission for homeless people, and it used to be some sort of bordello back during the Gold Rush. He'd renovated it to have a living area upstairs, and downstairs he'd put in a gun shop—obviously the perfect store for a raving mad lunatic to live above and not a recipe for disaster at all (insert eye roll here). My half-brother Caleb got his own room on the same floor as my dad and the evil stepmom. I got the pleasure of sleeping in the attic with the other "flowers," my two stepsisters and my half-sister, Samantha. I didn't mind sharing with them because it made the fact that the room was haunted a little easier to deal with. Caleb usually joined us because his room was the worst. The lights shut off and the door slammed for no reason. In our room, things just got moved around, so it was not as bad.

Anyway, I was pretty sure that would be one of the last times I had to stay there because I was thirteen and almost legally able to decide if I wanted to visit anymore. I was torn, though, because I knew I'd miss Caleb and Samantha.

I found out later from my first stepmom that the evil stepmom had been on the news because she'd held herself hostage in the gun shop. Apparently, she'd threatened to shoot herself or anyone else who dared to enter, so the SWAT team surrounded the rescue mission/gun shop/house/ex-bordello. I could just picture her sitting behind the cash register putting on lipstick with one hand and holding a Smith & Wesson in the other, making small talk with all of the creepy taxidermized animals. I couldn't believe my dad had found the one person on the planet that was crazier than him. She actually made him seem normal. Luckily, she chose to snap when Caleb and Samantha were at school. Eventually, she gave herself up, and the SWAT team cuffed her and took her away. I never saw her again.

Back in the present, I told Collin, "No, it's cool I guess."

What in the hell am I saying right now? He totally had me losing my mind. I hated smoking. I mean, really, *hate* was a mild word for how I felt about it. I loathed it. I was disgusted by it. I was repulsed by it. After my dad and the evil stepmom choking our dysfunctional Brady-bunch family with their non-stop smoking in the back of the sketchy looking camper van they'd had to buy to fit all of us in, and my ex-friend, Maeve, stealing cigarettes and tormenting me all through junior high, I should have gotten in my car and gone right then.

Did it bother me? Heck yeah! But I couldn't seem to resist him, smoking and all. *Why can't you think straight, Lindsay?*

"Hey, let's take my car to Lainey's since I just got it back from the shop. I'm totally stoked to drive," he said.

"Okay, awesome."

He took my hand and led me to his parked car. As he was about to unlock the door, he hesitated. "Wait, I need to do this first," he said and placed his hands on the car on either side of me and leaned in for a kiss. His mouth tasted like an ashtray, but I didn't pull back.

It felt dangerous and exciting, like I shouldn't have been kissing him but couldn't stop myself. We stayed like that for what seemed like an eternity until Collin finally released me after basically pinning me to his car.

"Are you hungry? I'm starving? Let's go in and grab some grub before we go," he said.

"I ate before, but that's cool if you're hungry. Lainey probably won't have any food. Well, maybe some Doritos, but that's probably it," I said with a chuckle even though it wasn't really funny. It must have been my nerves—my stomach was fluttering up to my throat, and I was doing my best to push it back down to where it belonged.

"Cool." Collin took my hand again, and we walked down a short path that curved around the building of cute cape-cod style condos painted pale gray with bright white trim. We got to the front door of his mom's condo, which was painted a darker gray, and Collin took out his keys and put the key in the lock but stopped with his hand still holding the doorknob.

"My mom and Christopher might still be home. They said they were going to the movies, but the light is still on," he said before turning the knob to open the door.

The door opened into the living room, and I could see where all of the family's artwork and tchotchkes had ended up. There was a fireplace to the right and above it a gigantic watercolor painting of a sailboat. Along the mantel were carved wooden birds perched on sticks of varying heights—sandpipers, I thought. Smack dab in the middle of the room was a daybed with a scrolled, white-painted iron frame posing as a sofa. There was an overstuffed floral chair in the corner and a small chestnut-brown side table only big enough for a lamp and maybe a cup of coffee. The room felt bigger than it was, probably due to the high ceilings. Before I could fully take in the space, a voice came from behind the wall that separated the living room from what appeared to be the kitchen.

"I thought you were going to a party. What, did you get hungry or something?" A woman with gray-streaked, straight brown hair cut into a chin-length bob and striking blue eyes popped out from behind the wall.

"Oh, hi! I didn't know we had company. I'm Collin's mom, Patricia," she said, rubbing her hand on her jeans and then reaching it out to shake my hand.

"Hi, I'm Lindsay," I said, shaking her hand.

"Collin, you didn't tell me how cute she was," she said, winking at me.

I could see where Collin had gotten his charm because it definitely hadn't been from his dad.

"Mom!" Collin said, exasperated.

"Thanks," I said, trying to keep my face from turning red.

"Anyway, Christopher and I are just about to go. There's leftover meatloaf in the fridge. You're welcome to have it as long as you clean up after yourself," she said, then turned toward the hallway to the left and yelled, "Christopher, let's go!"

Christopher emerged from the hallway saying, "Coming, jeez!" He looked nothing like Collin or his parents. He was about a foot shorter and two feet wider, with round rosy cheeks, a light brown buzz cut, and warm brown eyes. He noticed me standing beside Collin.

"What's up?" Christopher said, nodding his head.

He and Collin's mom took their jackets off the hooks by the front door.

"Alright, I just don't want to be late. Bye, it was nice to meet you," Collin's mom said, opening the door for Christopher.

"Bye, nice to meet you, too," I said, and she closed the door behind her.

"Ugh! I thought they would never leave. Okay, grub sesh time, where's that meatloaf?"

I followed Collin into the kitchen. It was a small galley-style kitchen with white cupboards and off-white tile counters. It was the complete opposite of his dad's dark, cave-like kitchen. While Collin was bent over digging through the fridge, I took a seat at the small round table on a spindly wooden chair painted a cheerful yellow.

"Hoo hoo!" Collin leaned back and howled. "Grub sesh!"

I giggled, which egged him on, and he started doing a full-on dance, flapping his arms, jutting out his chin, and stepping forward and back. His dance looked something like a cross between the funky chicken and the hustle, and then we were both cracking up.

I wished Lainey could have seen him now, he was so much fun. Bill Warner had never been like this. His idea of goofing around would have been watching *60 Minutes* instead of the *MacNeil-Lehrer NewsHour;* the only reason I knew about those two programs was because he'd made me sit and watch them with him while he'd cracked up.

"Can you believe they call this news?" he would have said, and I would have just nodded and smiled.

Collin was now heating up meatloaf in the microwave. "You sure you don't want any?"

"I'm sure. Do you have anything to drink?" I said.

"Uh, yeah." He went back to the fridge. "We have some Diet Coke, my mom's addicted." He took a can out and held it up.

"Okay, great! Thanks!"

He set it on the table in front of me. "Do you want a glass with ice? It doesn't seem that cold."

"Um, yeah, sure. Thanks!"

"Whoa! That gives me an idea." He began opening all of the cupboards, searching for something. "Ah, here it is! Saa-weet!" he said, reaching back into the cabinet over the fridge—which he could do, due to his six-foot-two-inch height and long arms. He pulled out a bottle of Bacardi rum and held it over his head, grinning from ear-to-ear and showing off his sparkling white teeth, like the bottle was a belt and he'd just won the World Heavyweight Championship.

"Uh, you don't think your mom will notice?" I said. Lainey's sister, Ava, once told us that their mom used to mark their bottles of liquor, so she used to fill them up with water back to the line after drinking from them so her mom wouldn't suspect anything. Lucky for Ava, her mom wasn't a big drinker, otherwise she might have noticed that by the time Ava graduated from high school, there was basically just water in those bottles.

"Nah, she doesn't even drink. She just swiped them from my dad in the divorce to piss him off. Look, it's all dusty," Collin said, setting it on the counter and taking out two glasses.

I already knew what was coming—we weren't going to Lainey's, and this might not end well, but I didn't speak up. I didn't speak up anymore, in general. I was afraid people wouldn't like me. The last time I'd spoken up had been back in elementary school, and I'd lost my best friend. I didn't want to lose any more friends or, worse, make enemies who would torment me at every turn. I did not want to live through that again.

Collin dug ice out of the freezer with his bare hand and plopped it into the two glasses, cracked open the Coke, poured some into each glass, and then topped off each drink with a generous amount of Bacardi. He opened a drawer, jingling its contents, pulled out a butter knife, and stirred the drinks with it. He took a sip of one of the drinks.

"Woo hoo, screamin'!" he said, raising the glass as if he was making a toast. "Here, try it!" He handed me the other glass.

"Cheers!" I said, and we clinked glasses.

nineteen

A Jacuzzi plus four rum-and-Cokes each plus a bag of Doritos equals disaster. I was hunched over the bushes behind the clubhouse of Collin's mom's condo complex, thinking there couldn't possibly be anything left in my stomach, when another wave of nausea washed over me, and I was heaving again. I was shivering but sweaty. I tried to keep hold of the towel that I had around me to cover my wet bathing suit. I saw Collin out of the corner of my eye sitting on the curb, smoking.

When my stomach finally stopped rebelling, I sat back on the sidewalk, leaned up against the wall, and closed my eyes. The spinning had stopped, too. All I could do was sit there, breathing. I heard Collin's footsteps padding on the grass.

"You good?"

"I've been better," I said.

"I think I should take you back to my mom's to sober up a bit."

"Don't you think your mom is back by now?"

"Yeah, but we can go through the garage, that's where my room is, anyway."

"Okay."

Collin hoisted me up and put his arm around my shoulders to help steady me like I was an injured football player coming off the field. He smelled like chorine, deodorant, and cigarettes. I was starting to get my sea legs back, but I let him keep helping me walk anyway. I couldn't remember his mom's condo having been so far away from the pool. It felt like we'd walked half a mile by the time we made it back to his mom's.

"Wait here." Collin disappeared around the corner, and then the garage door opened. I could see his flip-flopped feet through the opening. When the garage opened up to his board shorts, he ducked down under the garage door to collect me.

"Welcome to my humble abode," he said. He guided me to a black folding chair parked in front of an old-school, teacher-style metal desk, then closed the garage door. The garage was not as big as I'd pictured it—it was a one-car garage that had been converted to a laundry room/teen hideout. The desk marked the barrier between the laundry room and the hideout. In the hideout was an oval-shaped, red-and-blue braided rug and a futon with a black cushion and black metal frame.

I had stopped sweating but was still shivering, legitimately cold now. "I need to change my clothes. Where did I leave my bag?"

"I brought it in here when I went in to open the door." He reached down next to the futon and pulled up my pink duffel bag. When I stood up to take it from him, I lost my balance, and he caught me in an embrace.

I could feel the heat coming from his body. My legs were liquid, and I couldn't stand up. We were in a dance, and I was swaying. He was swallowing me up. There was music—I couldn't tell if it was only in my head. The smell of chlorine and the dampness were unbearable. I peeled off my swimsuit, which made me feel better. I wasn't standing anymore, but I couldn't remember falling. I felt softness under me, but I was not comfortable, as there was a weight on top of me. I closed my eyes. I wanted to sleep. I wanted to curl up. I wanted it to be quiet. I kept hearing music. I heard grunting. I heard knocking. It was cold. I opened my eyes. I saw Collin's mom. I saw Collin and his mom yelling at each other. *Am I having a bad dream?* I heard a door slam. *Get up!* My head was pounding. My body was naked. On my hands and knees, I searched— *Where are my clothes?*

Oh God, let this be a bad dream.

twenty

Monday

I was sitting with my back up against the wall between the stacks of books in the school library eating a granola bar I'd found buried in the bottom of my backpack. I had been hiding out all day. I didn't want to face anyone—not Collin and certainly not Lainey. I wasn't ready for her third degree on why I hadn't shown up to her house on Saturday night. I was still trying to process what had actually happened—and whether it was what I thought it was. I was horrified and could never face Collin's mother again. I just wanted to crawl in a hole and never come out.

I heard someone coming—*Shit!* I grabbed one of the books off the shelf and covered my face with it. I recognized Collin's vans pointed right at me.

"I thought I might find you in here," he said and dropped a note folded into a neat square onto my lap. "I know you're avoiding me."

"No, I just needed to do some research for a report," I said without lowering the book.

"Ah, yes, the big St. Bernard report for dog history class," he said, dropping his backpack on the floor and sitting next to me.

I closed the book to look at the cover. "Oops, busted."

"Will you just read the note?" he said.

I put down the book, took the note from my lap, opened it, and read it to myself.

Lindsay,

Happy Monday sweetie!!! I love you very much!!! I'm sorry about Saturday night sweetie – never happen again ok? Now since I'm with you why don't you look at me so I can kiss you...

I love You Sweetie!

Collin

I folded the note and looked at Collin. His eyes were searching mine for some kind of reaction. Maybe I should have just kissed him and forgotten about everything that had happened over the weekend. That was what my body wanted to do more than anything, but my brain had actually kicked in, and it was telling me, *Danger, danger, stay away, go back!*

"I think we need to talk first," I said, not knowing exactly where to begin. I stared at my shoes. I was still in shock.

"Okay. So you're still mad at me for getting you drunk."

"No, I'm not mad at you. I'm mortified that your mom walked in on us. At least, I think that's what happened. Isn't that what happened?" I looked at him out of the corner of my eyes.

"Oh, that. Yeah she was a little pissed, but not about that," he said and flopped his hair over with his hand. "I'm staying at my dad's again for a few days until she cools off."

"Oh my God!" I said and buried my face in my hands.

"She wasn't mad at you, though. She was mad at me for drinking the rum and not cleaning up the kitchen. She actually likes you," he said, flopping his hair over again. "She thinks you're a good influence on me." He chuckled.

"Yeah, she didn't see me puking my guts out," I said and looked at him again.

He was smiling a huge toothy smile that made the corners of his eyes wrinkle. "I'm sorry you got sick. I promise I won't let it happen again. Now, how about that kiss?" he said, then reached his hand to the side of my face and leaned in.

I smelled cinnamon on his breath. His lips were warm, and I forgot everything for a minute. I forgot that I was sitting in the school library. I forgot that I'd allowed myself to get so drunk that I'd let him have sex with me even though I hadn't wanted to. I forgot that his mom had walked in on us. I forgot that they'd had a fight. I forgot to care about anything anymore.

I managed to unlock my lips from Collin's just in time to sneak out to my locker before practice. I opened my locker, and a note fell out and landed at my feet. Before I even bent down to pick it up, I knew who it was from—Lainey. I could recognize her wild chicken scratch writing anywhere. I was pretty sure she was mad at me for not coming to her party and not calling her. I was almost afraid to read what she'd written.

I reached down to pick it up and saw that she'd called me Binsy, which was her nickname for me, and she'd taken the time to write it in its full version in all caps with an Asian-style bubble-letter design. I guess she wasn't as mad as I'd thought.

Binsychan –

Hey Hey Baby, wuzzle up? Well, what u've told moi, has told moi nothin'! Where the hell were you? So, did u or did u not say u were comin' to my soiree? What R u smokin'? J/K I guess U and Collin are pretty serious now!

Are you going to the formal or what? Well I hope so! AND u r right I was practically BARFING EVERYwhere, sorry had 2 let it go! NO Kidding! Know what I mean Jelly Bean? What R U gonna do tomorrow? Call me girly! We need to catch up!

Luv Ya!

Baineychan!

I looked at my watch, it had taken me a full five minutes to absorb her hieroglyphics. There was no time to find her now. I was definitely going to be late.

twenty-one

Tuesday

I stood barefoot in my driveway, washing my stepdad's black Mustang convertible. I shoved the giant sponge into the soapy bucket of water. It went in with a *thunk*, and soapy water splashed over the sides. Whoops. I lifted up the heavy, dripping sponge and started on the windows.

The day was quiet and still. There was no wind or birds chirping, even though it was warm. I zoned out as I made large soapy circles on the car, thinking about how no one had noticed that I was late to practice yesterday because our advisor, Ms. Surly, was busy handing out the picture order forms. However, Mr. Headstrong totally noticed that I was twenty minutes late for English today and locked the door on me. I couldn't believe it! Ugh! It was so aggravating. I'd had to waste even more time going to the office to get an admit slip and, since it was my third tardy in a row, a stinkin' detention slip. Lucky me. I had a good excuse, though. I'd had to make sure my hair was perfect this morning since we had cheerleading pictures. Seriously, this photo was going to be in the yearbook, people! I could not risk a bad hair day being immortalized for all to see. It was totally worth it.

I hadn't had a chance to break the detention news to my mom yet, thank God. She and my stepdad had rushed out the door to drive across the bay to their favorite restaurant for dinner. It was kinda weird for a Tuesday, but today was the anniversary of their first date or something like that.

I released the sponge to drop it back into the bucket, but I missed, and it splat right on the concrete. What the heck? Had the bucket moved by itself? Wait—I was moving—no, the ground was moving! Holy crap, we were having an earthquake!

I spun around to look at the street, and the blacktop was rolling in waves like the ocean. The parked cars were bouncing up and down. *Oh my GOD!* I turned around, ran into the house, and saw the dishes flying out of the cabinets. I stopped dead in my tracks at the doorway, remembering that I was not wearing shoes. My stepdad's expensive bottle of cognac, which usually had the seat of honor on my mom's lit-up bookshelf, hurled itself to the floor and smashed in about a thousand pieces, filling the room with the smell of alcohol. I felt nauseous at the smell since I still wasn't over what had happened the previous weekend. I had to brace myself in the doorway to not fall over.

When it seemed like the shaking had stopped, my legs still felt week. I sat down in the doorway. *What in the hell am I supposed to do now?* The sun was setting, and the house looked dark. I thought the power was out, but then the phone rang. I crawled through the living room, not ready to trust my legs. I stretched to reach the phone attached to the wall, then sat back down and leaned against the wall with my knees bent to avoid the broken glass. I put the phone to my ear.

"Hello?"

"Hello, Lindsay, it's Grandpa. Are you okay?"

"Hi, Grandpa, yes, I think so. Are you okay?"

"Your grandmother and I are fine. Do you want us to come over?"

"Yes. Everything is broken over here."

"Okay, stay put. We'll be right over."

"Okay, bye." *Click*

Thank God my grandma and grandpa lived close by. They had been following my mom around. Every time she moved, they moved. I didn't know what I would do without them. I loved being with my grandparents. They were funny, but not because they told a lot of jokes or anything. They were funny in the way they interacted with each other. They could have had their own sitcom. My grandpa came from a big Italian family that immigrated to New York, so he had a strong Brooklyn/Italian accent. My grandmother came from the south, and she didn't have a strong accent because she'd moved from Tennessee to Texas when she was really young, but she used these funny expressions all the time, so their conversations were crazy.

Grandma had a styled-once-a-week hairdo of short, blond, hot-roller curls, and she was, let's just say, full-figured. With all that southern cooking, those grits and that gravy will catch up with you. Grandpa, on the other hand, was thin as a rail, proof that the Mediterranean diet was the way to go. He always wore a brown leather cap when they went out. He was bald from scurvy due to his days as a sailor with the merchant marines.

One time, I was on a drive with my grandma and grandpa. As always, my grandma was driving, and my grandpa was sitting in the passenger seat, holding on to the handle above the car door window. I sat in the back. My grandma ran a stop sign. Luckily, no one was around.

My grandpa rose his hand, palm up, and shook it like he was flipping a pizza as he said, "She sees it, she doesn't care! She just goes right through!" Italians have to use their hands when they speak, it's an unwritten rule.

My grandma snorted and said, "Oh, Vinny, Bless your heart." This is basically like saying, "Screw you, jerk" in Southern.

I laughed, and they asked me what was so funny, which made me laugh even more. They had no idea they were funny, and I loved that about them.

I heard my grandparents pull up in their Volvo and slam their car doors shut. I had left the front door wide open in all of the chaos, so I could see them lumbering up our walkway. They were moving pretty fast for old people. My grandpa was holding a broom and dustpan.

"For Heaven's sake, Lindsay, where are your shoes, child?" my grandma said, holding the doorjamb as she hoisted herself up the single step. "Don't move. Vinny, she's not wearing shoes, you need to get in there and sweep this all up." She pointed her finger back and forth, motioning toward the kitchen.

"That's what I'm doing, Marie, why do think I brought the broom?" he said, walking past her and gesturing with the broom since his hands were full.

"Sorry, I was out washing the car, and—"

"Oh, don't you worry your pretty little head," Grandma interrupted, looking around the room and sniffing the air. "What on earth is that foul smell?"

"Oh, yeah, that. That was Chip's cognac he brought back from Japan."

"Good Lord, your mother is never going to get that smell out of the carpet! Here are your shoes, honey." She handed me a pair of my mom's loafers. I took them and put them on—now was not the time to argue about whose shoes they were. My mom and I wore the same size, anyway.

"Thanks, Grandma." I stood, using the wall to steady myself. I wasn't sure if my legs had finished wobbling. "Thank you both for coming over here so fast. I'll grab another broom and some garbage bags."

"Marie, why don't you try the TV?" my grandpa called from the kitchen.

"Alright, alright, now where is the remote?" She shuffled the newspapers and magazines on the coffee table and found the remote. "How do you work this newfangled thing?" she said, adjusting her glasses.

"Grandma, it's the same one you have."

"It is? Well, what do you know?" She snorted and laughed. She examined the remote and then turned on the TV. We all stopped what we are doing, frozen in our places in silence. The images from the screen frightened me. The entire Embarcadero Freeway in San Francisco had collapsed onto itself. You could see cars crushed underneath it. People were running around, and there were fire trucks and police cars everywhere. A woman on screen with a microphone was talking about casualties. My heart dropped to my stomach. My hands felt clammy. I felt like I might faint. My mind was working overtime. I was freaking out inside. Where had my mom and Chip said they were going again? Marin? Sausalito? I couldn't remember where, but it didn't matter, they still needed to take this freeway to get the Golden

Gate Bridge! My eyes welled up with tears—my mom and Chip could have been in there.

My grandma looked over at me and saw that I was crying.

"Oh honey, what's the matter?" she said, putting her arm around me. Just in time, too, as my legs were feeling woozy again like I might collapse.

"My mom," I said, "and Chip…" I was having trouble getting the words out between crying and trying to breathe, "…were driving across…the bay…for dinner." I started crying and gulping air.

"Now, now, don't go puttin' the horse before the cart. We don't know that they're in that mess. They probably went the other way," she said, giving me a reassuring squeeze.

"The goddamn traffic was probably a mess, due to that goddamned baseball game. They probably didn't even make it to the city yet. Probably still sitting on the one-oh-one," my grandpa said, gesturing in the direction of the freeway.

"You mean the World Series?" I said, trying to stop crying. "Wait…there's another way…to get to the Golden Gate Bridge?" I backed away from my grandma to look her straight in the face.

"I never liked the stinkin' Giants, especially when they were in New York, and I sure as hell don't like the A's." My grandpa swatted the air with his hand and mumbled on his way out of the room. "Ha! Figures we'd have an earthquake."

"Wait, Grandma, how else can you get to the Golden Gate Bridge?" I was calming down and finally able to get a complete sentence together.

"Oh, let's see. You take the ninety-one over yonder to two-eighty, but it'll take ya till the cows come home." She went to the sofa and sat down with a *plumff*. "I am plain worn out."

I had managed to stop crying. Maybe they hadn't been crushed to death. I said a prayer: *Dear God, please keep my mom and Chip safe, thank you so much, amen.*

The phone rang. My heart stopped, and I couldn't move. It was like I'd forgotten how to. A thousand things were running through my mind. Was it my mom calling to say she was fine? Was it the hospital? The police? Oh my God. What if it was the police?

"Linds, Linds, Lindser, LINDSAY!" Grandpa had to yell to get my attention. "It's for you, some kid. Says his name's Collin."

Oh my God. I'd totally forgotten about him. Ugh! I really didn't want to talk to Collin. I couldn't talk to him. I was so worried, I couldn't even think straight. It was nice that he'd called, though, and I guessed I should find out if he was okay.

I willed my legs to walk over to the phone, took the receiver from Grandpa's hand, and put it to my ear.

"Hello?"

"Hey, Lindsay! Whoa, some earthquake, right? What a trip! The whole house was jumpin'!" he said, sounding excited, like he'd just gone to some major party.

It irritated me that he could be so carefree at a time like this. Why wasn't he freaking out? Why wasn't anyone freaking out except for me? It seemed like that was all I did. I wasn't sure I even knew how to be calm.

"Collin, I gotta go. I need to keep this line open in case they try to call."

"In case who tries to call? Lind—"

I hung up on him. Wow, I couldn't believe I'd done that. He was probably going to be pissed about this—I would have been. But I wasn't thinking straight. To be honest, I hadn't been thinking straight since I'd met him. I wanted to be with him, but I couldn't.

I didn't know what to do with myself. I considered cleaning up—that could keep my mind occupied. I turned around to see that my grandpa had everything swept up.

"Thanks, Grandpa," I managed to say.

I walked back into the living room, and my grandma patted the sofa cushion, my cue to sit down next to her. I flopped down on the sofa and let her put her arm around my shoulders. I rested my head on her shoulder like I used to when I was five years old. I felt like I was five years old—totally helpless. There was nothing I could do that would change this situation. All I could do was wait, and it was killing me.

I shut my eyes tight to block out the images on the screen. I imagined I was walking through an open field, and there was nothing but tall grass in every direction, as far as the eye could see. The grass swayed in the breeze, and with each step I took, the grass flattened, forming a path behind me. I looked up at the sky. It was gray. I couldn't see any individual clouds—there was just one big gray cloud. I saw something on the ground. It was a rock, but it was shiny and gold—a gold nugget. I reached down to pick it up, but I couldn't. It was stuck to the ground. I saw something moving toward me out of the corner of my eye. It was small, dark, and low to the ground—a snake. It slithered toward me; it was coming so fast. I left the gold nugget on the ground, turned, and ran back through the flattened path I'd made. I was running and running and running. The grass disappeared, and I was left in the gray nothingness. I was falling. There was no place to land. I was just falling. I gave in to the fall, and then my entire body jerked to a stop, and I took a breath like it was the first time I'd ever taken a breath, with a giant gasp and a shiver.

"Well, someone must have just walked over your grave. Did you have a nice nap?" my grandma said. She always said that whenever anyone shivered. I didn't really know what it meant, but it made sense.

What didn't make sense was how I could have been asleep. I was so on edge, and I'd only closed my eyes for a second.

"What? Was I asleep?" I asked my grandma, sitting bolt upright.

"For about forty-five minutes," she said and clicked off the TV.

"Did they call?" I asked looking from one of my grandparents to the other like I was watching a tennis match and waiting for the winning shot.

"Not yet, honey. I'm sure they will any minute now," she said, setting down the remote and picking up her pen and crossword puzzle that were sitting on the coffee table.

"Are you hungry? What do you think you're gonna want for dinner?" She looked at me over her reading glasses.

"No. Nothing." My stomach was in a giant knot; I would probably vomit if I had to eat something.

The phone rang. I jumped up and then fell right back down, feeling lightheaded.

"I'll get it," my grandpa said as he shuffled toward the phone. Two more rings had gone by. "Hello?"

I finally got to my feet without falling over and ran to the phone. I put my head next to the receiver still in my grandpa's hand.

"Mom? Mom? Is that you?" I said, breathless.

My grandpa handed me the phone, giving me a look.

I mouthed the word *sorry*, and he swatted the air with his hand and walked back to the living room.

"Lindsay? Yes, it's me," my mom said.

"Oh, thank God, you're okay!" I said. A feeling of relief washed over me, and with that, the tears started again.

"What? Of course, I'm okay. Why are you crying? What's going on?" she said. She sounded so calm.

"We just had a major earthquake, and I thought you were dead, that's what's going on!"

"What? Oh, yeah, I thought I felt a bump in the road. We decided to take the two-eighty to avoid the World Series traffic by Candlestick, and Chip was going about a hundred miles per hour. While we were at the restaurant, they told us that they closed the bridges, so it looks like we'll be stuck here for the night," my mom said, like it was no big deal, like I hadn't just spent the last two hours worried sick. *A bump in the road—is she kidding me?*

"Okay, yeah. I'm just glad you're okay," I said, trying to remain calm. It was taking every ounce of energy I had left to control my frustration and keep my voice steady rather than letting it turn into a weird, high-pitched, whiney cry. "Grandma and Grandpa are here, and they helped me clean up."

"Clean up? Clean up what?"

"Mom, we had a seven-point-two-magnitude earthquake! All of the dishes came flying out of the cupboards!"

"Really, it was that bad?"

"Yes! And the Embarcadero Freeway collapsed!"

"Wow, okay. Well, I'll be home as soon I can. Maybe you should stay with them tonight," she said.

"I think I'll be okay. I was just worried about you and Chip," I said.

"Okay. Well, our room is ready, so I have to go, but I'll call you in the morning. Love you," she said.

Sometimes I think my mom was insane. Was I the only one in this family with the appropriate freak-out gene?

"Okay, love you, too." I hung up the phone and paused for a moment with my hand on the receiver, wondering what I should do next.

"Well, what'd she say?" my grandma asked.

Her voice startled me—I'd forgotten they were there. I turned to look at her and saw both grandparents staring at me.

"She said they closed the bridges, and they have to stay there for the night."

"Well, see, there you go. Everything is going to be fine. Do you want us to stay here, or do you want to come over to our house?" my grandma said.

I really just wanted to crawl in my bed; making decisions seemed like too much work.

"I'll be fine now. You don't have to stay. I have homework, and then I'm just going to go to bed early," I said.

"What about dinner?" my grandma asked.

She always worried about what I wanted for dinner. When I was in seventh grade, my mom and I got kicked out of our condo because the owner had wanted to sell and my mom couldn't find a new place right away. We went to live with my grandparents. My mom usually left before I woke up, so my grandma would make me breakfast, which was nice because when it was just my mom and I, I had to fend for myself. Anyway, my grandma asked me every day while I was eating breakfast what I thought I would want for dinner. I could never come up with an answer because, for one, I was still eating breakfast; two, I usually just made Cup-O-Noodles or Chef Boyardee during the week since my mom would still be at work; and three, if my mom made dinner, she never asked me what I wanted, as she didn't have time for that.

"Um, I'll just make a sandwich if I get hungry. It's fine," I said.

"Well, okay, but you call us if you need anything," she said, giving me a disapproving look.

"I will. Thank you," I said and gave her a hug. "I love you."

"I love you, too, honey," my grandma said and gave me a squeaky kiss on the cheek.

"Come on, Marie. I need to take my pills, and *Jeopardy* is going to be on in five minutes," my grandpa said, already halfway out the door.

"Alright, alright, hold your horses. I'm comin'," my grandma said, reaching down for her purse and making her way to the door.

"Bye, Grandpa," I called from the door.

"Bye, Lindser," he said and raised his arm in the air, continuing his beeline to the car.

I closed the door and leaned up against it for a moment to collect my thoughts. Oh my gosh, I had totally forgotten about Chip's car. I ran out after them and saw them driving away. I turned to look at the driveway, and everything was put away—the bucket and the sponge, and even the hose was coiled up in a neat circle by the faucet. The car was locked and dry— maybe a bit spotty, but definitely dry. My grandpa must have cleaned it all up while I was sleeping.

twenty-two

Wednesday

I was surprised I made it to class on time. I guessed going to bed at eight p.m. like a nine-year-old instead of midnight made it easier to get up in the morning. I had been afraid to take the freeway to school because of all of those overpasses. I had taken the side streets and only had to cross one tiny overpass. I'd prayed the entire time.

Not only was I on time, but I'd actually found a parking spot in the lot, which never happened. I usually had to park on the street and then hike up the hill to the main campus. Lucky for us, our school was built like a prison, all steel and cinderblock, so we still had school today. Even after a major 7.2 earthquake, there was not a crack to be seen anywhere in that giant metal box.

On Wednesdays, we had homeroom. I was kind of dreading it because I knew Collin would be there and he would be mad that I'd hung up on him. I saw him sitting in his seat with his head down reading a piece of paper on his desk. I took my seat in front of him.

"Hi!" I said to him, but he didn't respond—crickets. Great, he was giving me the silent treatment. I took out my notebook, scribbled down a note, gave it a quick fold in half and then in half again instead of my careful triangle style, and dropped it over my shoulder on to his desk.

Collin,

Hey, what's wrong? I'm sorry I hung up on you yesterday. It's just that my mom was supposed to be going across the bridge and I didn't know if she was ok. I hope you're not too mad at me.

Love,

Lindsay

I heard him opening the note and then I heard him writing. I could tell he was angry because he kept jamming the pen to the paper. He gave my shoulder a firm tap. *Oh boy.* He was really mad. This was it. He was breaking up with me. I pretended I was scratching my shoulder to grab the note. I took a deep breath, waited for our homeroom teacher to turn around and face the board again, and then opened the note.

> Yeah, I was hella pissed. That was a shity thing to do but I guess I understand why you would be worried. Not me though, I would have been happy if my dad never came back. I know how you can make it up to me, turn around and give me a kiss and then we can both smile.
>
> Love,
>
> Collin

Oh my God! No! I couldn't kiss him here. What could I do? I didn't want him to be mad at me, but I *could not* do that! Just then, the bell rang, and everyone shoved their binders and notebooks into their backpacks. This was my chance.

I turned around and leaned across his desk to give him a quick peck on the cheek. He grabbed my upper arms to pull me toward him and went in for a full make-out. My stomach felt like it was in my throat squeezing my lungs out of my body because I couldn't breathe. It was an uncomfortable familiar feeling. I couldn't breathe because I was holding my breath, hoping the kiss would be over soon. I closed my eyes to block it out, and a sudden flashback played in my mind.

I was five years old and standing in a dark, musty backroom completely naked, and a boy and his friend were there, just staring at me. The cool air on my exposed body caused me to hold my breath and close my eyes. They'd said if I showed them my privates, they would let me play with them. They'd said if I told anyone, something bad would happen. They'd said it was my fault. I knew it was wrong not to tell my mom, but somehow I felt like it was my fault and that I would get in trouble for taking off my clothes.

Something bad was happening. The room went quiet, and I felt someone staring at us as if their eyes were hands tapping me on the back. I pulled away and grabbed my backpack and notebook and ran out of the class before Collin or the teacher could say anything. That familiar pit in my stomach was back—an uneasiness, like my stomach was a cage and there was a bird trapped in it, flapping its wings trying to fly out.

I slowed down to a fast walk, keeping my head down, weaving through the bodies to get to my locker before my next class. Collin caught up with me. I didn't look at him.

"Hey, what happened in there? Why did you run away?" he said.

"I didn't want to be late for art again," I said and stopped to face my locker and fumble with the lock. I didn't want him to be mad at me, but I also didn't want to talk about why I'd run out. I couldn't talk about it. I didn't want to think about that part of my life. I felt my eyes welling up.

"Hey, Lindsay. Look at me. I thought you loved me, but it seems like you care more about your mom than me," he said, his arms crossed, his voice impatient and his eyes boring a hole into my head.

"What? No, it's not that." I turned to look at him. "I do love you. I just don't like to kiss in public. It makes me self-conscious."

"Who gives a shit about what anybody thinks?" he said, almost yelling. His eyes were glassy.

I hadn't seen him like this since his fight with his dad. I was frightened by his anger but at the same time drawn to him. I understood him. I understood what it felt like when people rejected you, when you were on your own. I was the only one he had. I felt like I could help him, and maybe he could help me.

"I know, you're right, but I can't explain it," I said, hoping he'd just drop it, and we could go back to how we had been before I'd hung up on him.

A group of freshman cheerleaders walked by, slowing down to give me a look. I waved with a fake cheerful smile that said, *I'm fine, keep walking*, and they did.

"You know, no one is going to love you like I do. We have a connection that no one else has. I know you feel it, too. Just tell everyone to fuck off! It's us against them," he said and pulled me in for a hug.

A thousand things were swirling in my head. Was this really what I wanted? Did I really want to tell everyone to fuck off? The scent of cologne and his warm sweatshirt were telling me that maybe I did. The lavender, woodsy smell of his cologne took me to another place, a place far away from here without hundreds of people whizzing by. I just wanted to stay nuzzled with my face on his chest like this forever.

Then the bell rang. I pulled away and noticed that we were the only two people left in the hallway. Oh crap! I was late, and I already had detention!

"I gotta go! I love you!" I said, already halfway down the hall. I didn't even put my notebook in my locker.

twenty-three

Thursday

When I got to school, I found this note wedged in my locker.

Lindsay,

I just felt like writing you a note. I was doing homework and just finished reading to page 122 so that's cool right? Lindsay, I swear to God <u>I love you so much!</u> You make me have the best feeling! I don't think I can stop loving you this much, just more to come. I miss you right now. I know it happened so fast, but it's also very true. Let's try to stop these stupid arguments and just hug and kiss me. I love it when you do! I hope you love it when I express my love for you too. I know your family and your grades are important to you but let's be glad we have each other because I think we have something really special going and we should both be happy. I love you with every part of my body and I enjoyed our time at the beach and even in the halls at school. I feel like never letting go of you because I love you so much when you do things like that with me. You are screamin' 1st degree and I don't want you to ever change the way you are!!! I am going to stop rambling now okay?

I Love You so much!

Collin

I folded it up and put it in my backpack and ran over to the parking lot. I didn't have time to find Collin because I had to meet my mom for a meeting that I didn't want to have. My mom had been pissed when she'd found out about my detentions. I say "found out" because I hadn't gotten a chance to tell her—the school had called her! So now, not only was she pissed about the detentions, she was double pissed that I hadn't told her about them.

"How come you didn't tell me you had detention?" she said, looking straight ahead, her cream-colored snakeskin pumps making angry clacking sounds each time they hit the hard, dark gray cement of the school corridor.

"I was going to, but we had an earthquake, remember?" I said, still in shock that she could be so calm about that and so angry about this.

"I don't like your tone, young lady. I had to leave work for this," she said.

She didn't like my tone? What the hell? Aaargh! I was so frustrated! I should have been allowed to have a tone! I wasn't the one who had picked this school thirty minutes away from home without traffic—more like forty-five minutes away with traffic. How did she expect me to get to school every day on time and still do cheerleading and homework? There were not enough hours in the day. I wanted to yell all of this at her, but instead I just kept my head down and said nothing. It wouldn't change anything, anyway.

"You know, Lindsay, you have been so moody lately. What's going on with you?" she said, just as she was pushing open the attendance office door, like I was really going to spill my guts right there in front of everyone.

"Nothing. I was just late. That's all," I said and followed her through the attendance office into the vice principal's office.

"Ah, Mrs. Sheehan and Ms. Trifling, I've been expecting you," Ms. Wright said. "Please have a seat." She gestured to the two empty chairs on the opposite side of her desk.

My mom had taken Chip's last name when they'd gotten married, so now we had different last names. It had been weird at first, but I'd gotten used to it.

Ms. Wright smoothed out the back of her form-fitting black skirt and sat in her leather office chair. Her short blond angled haircut and expensive-looking silk blouse said *Ad Exec,* but there she was in a tiny office overlooking a high school courtyard instead of the San Francisco city skyline.

"Hello, Ms. Wright," my mom said, extending her hand. I shoved my hands in the pockets of my jean jacket and sat down.

"Well, it seems like Lindsay has been having trouble getting to class on time. She has had six tardies in the last two weeks and now has two detentions. If she gets another detention, she will have to do Saturday school, and we all know no one wants to do that," Ms. Wright said, flipping through a file on her desk. I assumed she was looking at my file and this was all going down on my permanent record. "This is highly unlike her. Up until now, she has been a good student and a role model, she even worked here in the office last year. Is there something going on at home that I should know about?"

Oh boy, she'd gone there. I thought for sure my mom would lose it over that comment. I was surprised she'd thought I was a good student. I mean, I was a good student, I got A's and B's, but she must not have gotten to the part in my file that explained why I'd worked in the office last year.

I came marching in here my junior year the day my chemistry teacher, Mr. De Meano, called me dumb in front of the whole class. Well, he didn't use those words exactly. He was up there by the white board with his tweed sport coat and thick glasses, writing down some formula we were supposed to use in our next experiment. He just wrote it but didn't explain it at all. He just said, "Okay, class, you'll be using this formula," then told us to get with our groups and start working. So I raised my hand to ask what we were trying to figure out with said formula, and it must have sounded like I was being sarcastic, but I was totally serious.

Then Mr. De Meano said, "There's Trifling back there asking another one of her dumb questions."

There was some nervous laughter from the other students. I was so humiliated and angry, I knew if I stayed in that classroom one more second, I would either scream or cry or both. So I picked up my binder, put it in my backpack, put my pen in the front pocket, got up, hoisted my backpack onto my shoulder, and walked out. Just before I turned to walk down the hall, I caught a glimpse of the class, and everyone was frozen with their mouths hanging open.

I kept walking straight to the office to talk to my grade level academic counselor. I blurted out the whole story to her in one breath, fighting back tears.

"Whoa, whoa, whoa. Take a deep breath, slow down, what happened?" she said.

I took a deep breath, which released the flood of tears I was holding back. She handed me a tissue. I repeated the story again, trying to get the words out, but I kept making involuntary deep hiccupping breaths like a toddler after a tantrum. She put on her glasses that were hanging around her neck on a silver chain, tapped her computer mouse, and began tapping at the keyboard.

"Well, let's just take a looksee here at your schedule. Maybe we can transfer you to a different class. Hmmm," she said. "Well, Mr. De Meano is the head of the science department, and he teaches all of the chemistry classes, soooo that's not going to work."

My tears came back at the thought of having to be tormented by this man for the rest of the year. Ms. Angelopoulos looked away from her computer, saw me crying again, and patted my hand.

"Now, now, honey, no need to cry. We're going to figure this out," she said with a big reassuring smile that revealed the large gap between her front teeth. "You just stay put, I'll be right back."

Ms. Angelopoulos got up from her chair and hobbled over to the principal's office. Before I even had time for a full recap in my head of all the condescending comments from my teachers over the years, she came out of the office and hobbled back over to her desk.

"Well, good news! Mr. Grosso has cleared you to drop chemistry and take physics next year," Ms.

Angelopoulos said and took off her glasses, letting them hang from their chain again.

"Really? Wow, thank you! But I thought chemistry was a pre-requisite for physics."

"Well, normally it is, but since your math grades are decent and you only need two years of a science to graduate, he was able to waive that requirement," she said.

I couldn't believe it! There must have been some reason why this had been approved so fast, without anyone even having to talk to Mr. De Meano or my mom. I probably hadn't been the first student to complain about him. I bet if I made a big deal about it, I could probably have gotten him fired, but seriously, who had time for that? I was just relieved that I didn't have to take chemistry.

Wait, what did I have to take instead?

As I was about to ask Ms. Angelopoulos, she said, "So, more good news! I was able to get Mr. Grosso to allow you to fulfill your community service requirement by working with me here in the office! Isn't that great?" She looked at me with a big, open-mouthed smile and her arms outstretched, prepping for a hug.

"Ummm, yeah, that's great!" I said and let Ms. Angelopoulos hug me.

Back in the present, my mom looked at me with a raised eyebrow and then at Ms. Wright, then said, "No, everything is great at home."

She couldn't say why I was late because it would have revealed we didn't actually live in the district. My mom had gone to visit the school that I was supposed to attend when we'd first moved here. She had been walking through the hall to the office, and a group of scary looking boys had whistled and cat-called her, so she'd turned right around and left the school. She'd thought that if they were doing that to a middle-aged woman, what would they do to a teenage girl? She figured this school would be better because it was surrounded by million-dollar homes, and since her cousin lived in the district, we could use his address to get in the school. Little did she know, rich kids also came with their own set of problems.

"Oh, well, that's a relief to hear," Ms. Wright said and adjusted her flipped-up collar. She thrummed her long red fingernails on her desk. "What do you propose we do about this situation?" She looked at me, and I crossed my arms over my chest and looked out the window.

My mom totally surprised me and went into this long rant about how I was a good student and a cheerleader and that I had a job and that they gave too much homework and not enough time to do it and not enough time to walk to class or eat lunch, and don't get her started on chemistry.

I turned to look at my mom. Where had she been keeping all this pro-Lindsay talk all this time? I was stunned, and I think Ms. Wright was, too. She was stammering, trying to get a word in, but my mom was not having it.

The bell rang, and everyone was pouring out of the halls, scrambling to get to their next class. I felt obligated to say something.

"I'll try harder to make it to class. The bell rang. Can I go now? I'm going to be late again." I didn't want to look at either one of them because I felt my nose prickle and my eyes water.

"Well, that's a start. I'll write you a note," Ms. Wright said and pulled out a stack of permit slips from her desk drawer. It was clear that this little meeting was over, and we all wanted out of her office. She couldn't write fast enough. She ripped the note from the pad and handed it to me.

"Thanks," I said, and my mom and I stood up to leave.

"Thank you, Ms. Wright." My mom extended her hand to her, and they shook hands.

"Of course," Ms. Wright said and nodded at my mom.

I just wanted to get out of there and avoid talking to my mom. I knew she was about to unload her wrath on me.

As soon as we stepped out of the office, my mom said, "You owe me. We'll talk about this when we get home."

"I know," I said.

twenty-four

The rest of the day was completely uneventful. Mr. Bello, my physics teacher, was totally cool. I had known that he would be, he was always cool. I think he may have been the last remaining hippie from the sixties. He'd gone to Berkeley, had a grayish brownish scraggly beard, and wore Grateful Dead t-shirts most days. Other days, he would change it up and wear t-shirts with funny science sayings on them. Today, he was wearing a t-shirt that said *Don't Let Gravity Get You Down,* and that was just what I'd needed to see. It reminded me of the one day when he was talking about center of gravity, and he mentioned that women have a lower center of gravity then men and that made it impossible for a woman to stand up against a wall and bend over and touch her toes. I couldn't believe this. I had been taking dance my whole life, and I was pretty sure I could do it.

He was sure I couldn't do it but said, "Okay, Lindsay, give it a shot. I've got to see this."

"I know I can do it," I said.

"Wait, wait, wait, we should place a bet. What should we bet?" Mr. Bello said and looked at the class. "Any takers?"

"How about everyone gets ten extra credit points if she does it," Harrison Garret, the boy genius, shouted out from the back of the room. He was a freshman and in physics already; he was probably going to graduate early because they would run out of classes for him to take.

The class cheered at his idea.

"Alright, how about five extra credit points. Deal?"

"Deal!" I said and walked up to the front of the class to find a blank spot on the wall, which was challenging because Mr. Bello was somewhat of a hoarder. There was stuff all over the place—skeletons of humans and animals, jars of pickled things in liquid, and stacks of books.

Mr. Bello moved Joe the skeleton out of the way. "How about here?" he said.

"Okay, here I go," I said and started to bend forward.

"Wait—drum roll, please," he said, and the class started drumming on the tables with their hands. "Okay, now!"

I bent forward, making sure to keep my legs pressed against the wall. I got to the halfway point.

"I'm nervous, don't hurt yourself," Mr. Bello said and pretended to chew his nails.

I kept going, and when I got my hands about two inches from the floor, I lost my balance and had to lean forward to catch myself. Then I adjusted so I was fully bent over with my face to my knees and toes touching.

The whole class groaned, "Awwwww!"

"Wow, that was impressive. You actually almost did it! I've never seen anything like it!" he said while I was still in the position. "I think you earned those extra credit points, give her a hand."

The whole class cheered, and I unfolded and did a curtsy. I walked back to my seat and high fived everyone on my way.

Today, I handed Mr. Bello my tardy slip.

"Thank you kindly, Ms. Trifling. Glad you could make it. We missed you," he said like he actually meant it.

"You're welcome, and thank *you*," I said. I wished all teachers were like him.

There was a note on the door. Cheer practice had been cancelled due to some family emergency of Ms. Margo, our advisor. I wasn't sure why we needed her there anyway because she also taught math and usually just sat on the floor in the back grading papers. She didn't do a lot of advising, but she had advocated for me when it had been time to vote for our captain. It had been between Charlotte and me. She'd had us give these little speeches as to why we would make a good captain. I'd talked about how I had experience going to competitions when I was on drill team and what it takes to win. I guess she'd liked that idea, as she said she could help us apply to competitions. It had gotten everyone excited, and I think that was why they voted for me. We had ended up winning the Superior Award at cheerleading camp over the summer, but that had been the end of our competitions. The excitement had fizzled out after that. The only really good thing that had come out of it was that Charlotte and I became a really great team. I had sensed she was taking it hard that she hadn't gotten to be captain, so I'd decided that we would be unofficial co-captains and had her work with me to choreograph our routines and teach them to the rest of the squad. This seemed to keep the peace, and we became friends because we spent so much time together.

The note on the door was a disappointment. I had been hoping practice would have gone late so my mom would have been too tired to talk. I was dreading going home. I did not want to hear a lecture.

I bumped into Charlotte on my way down the stairs.

"Practice is cancelled," I said.

"What, why?" she said, flipping her long blond curls behind her shoulders.

"Ms. Margo had a family emergency," I said with a hint of annoyance. We had a big game coming up, and we needed to finish our routine today so we had time to clean it up the rest of the week.

"Huh, that's too bad. We have the big game coming up," she said, reading my mind.

"I know, it really sucks."

"Can't we just practice anyway?"

"The door's locked. We won't be able to use the mirrors."

"That's fine. We're just learning routine, we don't need to see ourselves yet."

"Yeah, you're right. We should just practice on the lawn until it gets dark. I have a boombox in my car. I'll go get it."

"Okay, I'll wait here to let the other girls know."

"Awesome, be right back," I said and headed toward the parking lot. Just as I was rounding the corner, I bumped into Collin.

"Hey, Dimples, I thought you had practice," he said and opened his arms for a hug.

"I did—I mean, I do. Ms. Margo's not here, so I'm going to get my boombox. We're going to practice on the lawn until it gets dark," I said and went in for the hug. God, he smelled good. It was that woodsy smell that made me want drop everything and stand there hugging him for the rest of my life.

"It's gonna be dark soon. I can wait for you, and then maybe you can come hang at my dad's for a while. He's away on a business trip," he said and backed out of the hug to look at me while still holding on to my shoulders.

Wow, that sounded amazing and the perfect way to stay away from home. "Yes, that would be awesome. I'll meet you at your car."

"Sweet!" he said and went in for a kiss, but I cut it short even though I could have stood there forever.

"Okay, I'll see you soon," I said and ran down the corridor toward the parking lot to grab the boombox.

It turned out that we were only able to practice for about forty-five minutes, the sun set so early. But I was itching to be with Collin, so I said my goodbyes and took off for the parking lot, where he was waiting for me.

"I'll follow you," I said. I had only been to his dad's house the one time, so I wasn't sure how to get there.

"Great, let's go," he said.

twenty-five

After about twenty minutes of winding, hilly roads, we pulled into his dad's driveway. The house looked even more looming than I'd remembered. It almost looked haunted. All the windows were dark, and there was only one lone porch light on. If not for that light, it would have been totally pitch black.

Collin opened the garage, and we walked up the back steps to the dark family room. Collin fumbled to find the light switch.

"Hey, I have a surprise for you," he said and went to open the sliding glass door to the empty patio.

"Really, what?" I said, trying to keep my voice steady, unsure what kind of surprise could be out there, in the dark, with who-knows-what critters lurking in the shadows. Of course, I wasn't not going to let him know that I was nervous about whatever it was.

"This!" he said and produced a sandwich baggie with what looked like two stubby cigarettes in them.

"Oh, I don't smoke," I said. I guessed I should have been clearer about that when we'd first met.

"It's not cigarettes, they're joints. It's pot," he said.

"Yeah, no thanks. I don't smoke pot or do drugs," I said

"Come on, Lindsay, you drink alcohol and caffeine, and technically those are drugs."

"Yeah, but they're not *drugs* drugs, they're legal *technically*," I said.

Wow, this was hard. I didn't want to seem like a prude, and I wanted him to like me. He seemed so excited to share this with me, but I really didn't want to do this. I was having flashbacks to when Maeve and I had broken up.

Collin sat down on the step to the patio and motioned for me to sit next to him.

"I promise you'll love it. It's like alcohol, but you don't get sick, and you sleep like a baby," he said as I sat down next to him. "Don't you trust me? You know I care about you more than anyone else." He took one of the joints out of the baggie. He leaned back to pull a lighter out of his front pocket. He put the joint to his lips and lit it, taking a huge hit. He held his breath, and as he exhaled, a giant puff of skunky smelling smoke came out. He held out the joint for me to take.

"Your turn," he said with a huge toothy smile.

"I don't know."

"Come on, it'll be fun. Plus, you may not even feel anything the first time you try it. I didn't," he said.

I could sense that he was getting annoyed with me. "Okay fine," I said. Maybe I wouldn't feel anything and he would stop pestering me about it and we could just be together. I didn't want to start another argument. I took the joint from his fingers and held it with my index finger and thumb. I put it to my lips. I breathed in and coughed uncontrollably. He started laughing and took the joint from my fingers.

"Happens every time," he said, still laughing.

"Ugh, that's disgusting," I said when I finally regained my composure.

"You'll get used to it. Here, watch me." He did the whole "breathe in, hold it, blow it out" thing again. "Try again."

"I don't think I will ever get used to this, but okay," I said and tried to do the same thing he'd done. That time, I managed to do it with slightly less coughing. My throat was burning, and my eyes were watering. "Can I get a glass of water?"

"Good idea, and I'm starving, too. Let's raid the fridge," he said, taking one more hit then crushing out the joint. He hoisted himself up and reached out his hand to help me up. We walked back through the sliding glass door into the kitchen. Collin bumped into the sofa.

"Jesus Christ. It's so goddammed dark in here," he said and laughed. He was pretending to be blind, walking with his arms out. He stumbled toward me and pulled me in for a hug.

My throat was still burning, and I really needed that water, so I hugged him and then reached for the light switch.

"Oh yeah, we need sustenance," he said and let me go. He went to the fridge and pulled out a bunch of stuff. I started looking through the cabinets to find a glass. *Bingo.* I pulled a glass from the cabinet and filled it with tap water.

"I'm making a sandwich, hoo hooo!" he announced and howled. We both cracked up. "You want one?"

I wasn't really feeling anything from the pot—I guessed coughing it out instead of inhaling it had been a good thing—but it was 5:30, and I was starting to get hungry. I suddenly realized that I should have been home by now.

"Yes, but I think I have to go. My mom's already mad at me," I said. I really didn't want to go home, but I knew I shouldn't have been here doing this, especially on a school night.

"You can't go now. Screw her. Just call her and tell her you're at the library studying with Lainey," he said.

"Ha, ha, yeah. Lainey studying, that's not a huge red flag or anything," I said. My mom would definitely have known something was up. "I'll just say *I'm* at the library studying. Can I use your phone?"

"Yeah, it's over there," he said, motioning with his arm, his head back in the fridge.

I saw the phone siting on a small table next to the sofa. I hoped I would get the answering machine because I didn't think I could lie if she was actually on the phone. I dialed, saying a prayer to myself. It rang and kept ringing. That was a good sign. The answering machine picked up.

"You have reached 257-2530, we are unable to take your call, but if you leave your name and number, we'll get back to you as soon as possible." *Oh, thank God! What do I say? Keep calm, keep calm.* "Beeeeep!" *Oh, crap!*

"Hi, Mom, it's Lindsay. I had some research to do for a paper, so I'm at the library. I got a sandwich from Esposito's, so I don't need dinner. I'll be home by eight o'clock. Bye." I hung up the phone. Oh man, I hoped she bought it.

"Hey, Lindsay, you want turkey or ham or turkey and ham? I'm goin' smorgasbord over here! Woo hoo! Screamin'!" Collin called from the kitchen.

"Yeah, that sounds good," I said. I was actually getting pretty hungry. I went back into the kitchen to help make the sandwiches. He was making a total mess. There were, like, five different knives out, the lunchmeat was on one side and the bread was on the other. He stopped for a minute in the middle of the kitchen holding a butter knife with a glob of mayo on it, squinting his eyes, and scratching his head with his free hand.

"I'm so stoned," he said and started laughing. "Where's my sandwich?"

I started laughing. "Here, let me help you," I said and took the mayo'd knife out of his hand, finished the sandwiches, and put all the stuff back in the fridge.

"Duuuuude! You're a lifesaver!" he said. There didn't appear to be a dining room table, so I took our plates to the coffee table and went back to get Collin, who was still scratching his head.

"Come on, sit down," I said. We started eating our sandwiches.

Collin was eating like he has been on a deserted island for the past ten years. He was moaning, "Oh, this is so good!" over and over, and I couldn't stop laughing. Finally, he finished and took a giant gulp of my water. The next thing I knew, we were making out.

"Wait," he said and stood up. He took my hand. "Come with me." I got up and followed him down the dark hallway.

"Where are we going?" I said, not sure I could handle any more surprises.

"You'll see," he said and stopped and opened the door to a large bedroom. He turned on the light. It looked big enough to be the master, but I knew it wasn't because it had one unmade queen-sized bed, one dresser with some of the drawers open, clothes on the floor, and a Metallica poster on the wall. Something told me that Mr. Edward Vance, III, President of Golden State Bank, would never have left his bed unmade, let alone have a Metallica poster.

"Tada!" he said and gestured with his arm like he had just performed a magic trick.

"Awesome!" I said.

He turned off the light and pulled me toward him while inching toward the bed. I knew I shouldn't have been doing this. I had a whole list of reasons why this was a bad idea: *It was Thursday. I had school tomorrow. I had homework. He was wasted. My mom was already mad at me. I would probably be grounded. I could lose my car and have to take the bus again.* It was such a long list, but I was ignoring it. I felt an energy coming from him, it was like a giant magnet pulling me toward him. My brain was no match for the strength of it. I felt so many things pulsing through my body that I couldn't explain—excitement mixed with fear mixed with longing and sadness.

My clothes were now mixed with his on the floor. I was lying flat on my back staring up at the ceiling with the sheets bunched up at my feet and his arm resting across my bare body. He had fallen asleep. I lifted his heavy arm off of me and got up from the bed. I found all of my clothes and put them back on. I walked out of the room in search of a bathroom to check my appearance. I didn't want to explain bedhead to my mom in addition to why I was so late. I went back to Collin's room to say goodbye, but he was out cold. I pulled the sheet and blanket over him and slipped out the front door, locking it behind me.

It was so dark even the porch light wasn't helping much. I got in my car and locked the door. I wasn't really sure how to get out of there, but I figured if I kept going downhill, I'd get to a street I knew. It seemed like it took forever, but I finally made it to the main street. The clock in my car said 8:00, and I knew I had missed the arbitrary time I'd set for myself to be home. Whatever, my mom was already mad.

twenty-six

I pulled up to the curb in front of my house. I took a deep breath and got out of the car. I locked the door and went over in my head what I was going to say. I'd tell her that I'd gotten my research done but now I needed to write the first draft. Hopefully, she'd just let me go up to my room. I unlocked the front door, and my mom was sitting on the sofa reading a book.

"Have a seat," she said and gestured to the sofa across from her.

"Mom, I have a lot more work to do. Can I just go up to my room?" I said and readjusted my backpack on my shoulder.

"Sit," she said, pointing to the sofa and slamming her book closed.

"Ugh! Fine!" I said, dropping my backpack by the door and flopping down on the sofa. Here we go. There was no escape now. She used to just send me to my room when I was little. There hadn't been these long lectures. I would have gone to my room and laid on my bed holding my Raggedy Ann doll until I fell asleep, and magically when I woke up everything would have been back to normal. I was used to soothing myself. Since she had been married to Chip, they'd gotten into this New-Age, talk-it-out business, and it made me feel uncomfortable. I would rather not talk about anything. I just wanted it to go away.

"What's gotten into you lately?" she said.

"What do you mean?" I asked. I mean, seriously, so I'd been late a few times. I was still getting good grades, I'd been working a part-time job once a week, I was the captain of the pom pom squad, not to mention we'd had a major earthquake that had screwed up the freeways—of course I was going to be late a couple of times.

"Is there something going on that I should know about?" she said.

"No, nothing's going on. The freeway is messed up, and I have a lot of stuff to do. That's it!"

"You just seem moody."

"I'm a teenager!" I said, raising my voice. I was so frustrated with this conversation. I didn't want to talk about this anymore. "I'm fine." I said in a calm voice, realizing being calm might be the best way to end this interrogation.

"Well, if you won't talk to me about it, I need you to talk to a counselor," she said.

"What?" I yelled and jumped up. "You can't be serious!"

"I'm very serious, and I've already scheduled an appointment for you."

"No, I'm not going! I have practice and work and the game this Friday!"

"I made it for Saturday, and if you don't go, I will be forced to put you on restriction," she said.

Ugh! There it was, I'd known she would say that. Maybe Collin was right, he was the only person who understood and cared about me. How could she have done this? It was so unfair. I couldn't stand to be in the room with her for one more second. I grabbed my backpack and ran up the stairs to my room and slammed the door. I was so angry! I threw my backpack on the floor and paced back and forth like a lion in a cage. Why was I so angry? Why had she done this? I felt like screaming, but I couldn't, I actually still had homework.

You know what, fine, she can force me to see the stupid shrink, but she can't make me talk.

twenty-seven

Friday

Well, I managed to calm down enough to finish my homework, but it was probably 11:30 before I was able to go to bed. I also couldn't hit the snooze button in the morning because I had to wash, blow dry, and curl my hair so I could look presentable for the game after school. I was so tired that I had to drink a Diet Coke for breakfast. Then I was awake, but barely, and my stomach was in a giant knot.

And then I saw Collin before school in the parking lot.

"Hey, Dimples, that was a great last night. I slept like a baby, woo hoo!" he said and gave me a hug.

"Yeah, it was fun," I said, remembering my "talk" with my mom as I responded, so my voice came out flat, bordering on annoyed.

"Are you mad at me?" he said and released me from the hug to look at me.

"No, I got into an argument with my mom. She's making me go to a shrink. Can you believe it?" I said and dropped my backpack and gym bag to the ground because I couldn't deal with all that weight—it was just adding to my aggravation.

"What a bitch! Why?" he said.

"Because I've been tardy and have two detentions," I said.

"That's nothing. My mom tried to send me once, but I didn't go. Just blow it off!" he said and flipped his hair back.

"No, I can't, I just need to get it over with so she will leave me alone."

"You should come over after school, and we can smoke pot and forget about all this bullshit," he said and pulled me in for a hug.

"I can't, I have the game against Sequoia. Maybe we can meet up after?" I said and hugged him back.

"You should blow that off, too! Don't you want to be with me?" he said and put his hands on my shoulders to look in my eyes.

I looked away to avoid his hypnotic green eyes. "Yes, more than anything, believe me, but I can't just not show up to a game, I'm the captain, they'll kick me off the squad!" I said, and the bell rang. "Shit, I gotta go!" I reached down and grabbed my backpack and gym bag and hoisted them both onto my right shoulder to make my run to class easier.

"Wait, I need a kiss first," he said.

"Collin, I really need to go, I can't have another detention. I'll get Saturday school."

"No, you can't go until I get a kiss!" Collin grabbed my arm so hard it hurt. Why did he do this to me? He was so understanding one minute and so infuriating the next.

"Owwww, that hurts. Fine." I gave him a quick kiss, yanked my arm from his grasp, and ran to class. Luckily, I made it before the teacher closed the door.

Now my stomach was really upset. I felt like I might actually throw up.

Had that just happened? I couldn't hear a word the teacher said the entire class. I was too busy obsessing over everything that had happened in the last twelve hours. I was like a cheerleading zombie the rest of the day, walking through the halls smiling at people while my brain was checked out. Lainey saw me at lunch staring at my locker.

"Hey, Lindsay, whaz up, chikita?"

"Oh, hey, Lainey."

"Girl, you don't look so good. Here, have some of my bagel."

"Thanks," I said and realized I was starving. I tore off a chunk of it and stuffed it into my mouth.

"Whoa! That bad, huh!" she said, and I nodded, trying to choke down the giant bite.

"Yeah, my mom's on my case about being tardy all the time. She's making me go to a shrink, and I think Collin is mad at me now, too," I said, my voice muffled with the mouthful.

"You know what you need? A party! I'm having some people over after the game—you should come. We miss you. I feel like I haven't seen you since the beach the first day of school!" she said.

It was true. I really hadn't hung out much with my friends at all.

"Okay, that sounds good. I'll be there. Thanks for the bagel."

twenty-eight

Still Friday

It was sunny, the football team was on the field, the stands were packed with people, we were all wearing our cheerleading uniforms, my hair was curled, and my lipstick was on, but I was on autopilot. I was doing the moves, but I wasn't saying the words. I felt like I was in some cheesy horror film, where everything seemed normal and everyone was happy and cheering, but my ears were ringing and everything was going in slow motion. I wasn't feeling super cheerful.

I was scanning the stands, hoping to see Collin up there somewhere. I saw Lainey, Anna, and Jess. We made eye contact, and they waved, so I waved back. I mean, I didn't want to be rude, but I had really been hoping Collin would have been there so we could have talked after the game. I wasn't sure what he was thinking. Had he really been mad at me earlier when he'd grabbed my arm? Was that why he wasn't here? I knew this wasn't really his scene, but I'd thought he would have come because I was here. Maybe he didn't want to be with me.

I realized the rest of the squad had moved off the track to collect their pom poms for the halftime show, and I was standing on the track by myself.

"Lindsay, you comin'?" Charlotte yelled.

Everyone on the squad was looking at me like I had two heads.

"Yeah, sorry. I was just…." My voice trailed off—I saw Collin in the stands with Dan the pothead surfer. Oh my God! He was here! I got a sudden surge of adrenalin. "I'm coming!" I said and ran to grab my pom poms and then over to the band director to remind him of the song we were using.

This was the only thing that I didn't like about home games—we had to use band music instead of a tape. Normally that was okay, but this band was unpredictable, they played the music about a half count too slowly, and there weren't very many band members, so it wasn't really loud enough. We also had a limited list of songs to choose from. The band director gave us a list of, like, ten songs. Back at my other high school, the band had been huge and really good, so we hadn't minded dancing to their music. This band was kind of lame.

Anyway, I'd chosen "Barbara Ann" by the Beach Boys. I figured it was the easiest song on the list, so hopefully they wouldn't screw it up. I had been

LISA WOOMER

begging them all week to try to speed it up just a little. Well, I should have been careful what I'd wished for, because as soon as the first three notes hit the air, I knew we were screwed. It was so fast, we were scrambling to keep up. Charlotte and I were exchanging confused looks and then finally just burst out laughing because it was so ridiculous. It was like watching a video in fast forward. When we got to the part where we were supposed to do the pom pom pass—it was a repetitive move, but each time the girl behind you took your pom poms, the last girl tossed them behind her until everyone was pom pom free—the pom poms were flying, and we could barely contain ourselves. The next move, we had to link arms for a kick line. We were in height order with little Lana, who was about 4'9", at the end. She fell over, and because we were all attached, she brought us all down. By then, the whole crowd was laughing, too. It was basically a cheerleading disaster. We sat there on the ground laughing until the song finally ended and put us out of our misery.

The crowd cheered louder than I'd ever heard them. The band director was my least favorite person at that moment. He was over there smiling, giving me a thumbs up.

"Fast enough for ya?" he yelled across the field with his hands cupped around his mouth.

Jerk. I would have liked nothing more than to give him the finger, but instead I gave him a fake smile and a thumbs up.

After the game, I hightailed it off the field, mortified by our halftime performance. I didn't wait for anyone and headed straight to the locker room to change. Then I headed to the parking lot for the solace of my car. I was hoping that good old teenage amnesia would kick in over the weekend and everyone would forget about the game. I was basically power walking, going just shy of a slow jog, when I heard my name. *If I don't turn around, maybe they will think I can't hear them.*

Then I heard a group of people call my name together, and then Lainey's voice.

"We know you can hear us!" she yelled.

I stopped walking and just stood there, still not facing them. Lainey jogged up next to me. She bent forward, put her hands on her knees, and caught her breath.

"Lainey, I need to go," I said.

She held up her pointer finger, indicating she needed a minute. "Wow, I am really out of shape," she said, then stood up straight and pretended to stretch. "Where are you going so fast? I thought you were coming over to my house for a *PAR-TAY*!"

"I know, I'm sorry. I have had *the* crappiest week topped off by *the* most humiliating performance of my life. I am not in the mood to *PAR-TAY*."

"Oh, come on, it wasn't that bad. Besides, after one shot of Peppermint Schnapps, you'll forget all about it," she said.

Ugh! Just the mention of Peppermint Schnapps made me want to vomit. I couldn't believe she was still drinking that nasty cough-syrup tasting stuff. Didn't she remember what had happened the last time? Her older sister, Ava, had come home from college and brought her the leftovers from her last party, figuring no one smart enough to be in college would drink that crap. A week later, Lainey invited just a few of us over. It was supposed to be just Lainey, Anna, Jess, Lainey's cousin Danny, a couple of his friends, and me, so like eight people total. Well, somehow it got out that Lainey was having a party, and the next thing we knew, carload after carload of people were showing up at her house and pushing their way in. There had to be at least two hundred fifty people in her house. There were so many people we didn't even recognize half of them. I might have been the only sober person in our original crew because, like I said, Peppermint Schnapps was gross. Jess had a few shots of it and spilled something on her shirt. She went to the upstairs bathroom to clean up and then accidently locked herself in the bathroom in her drunken stupor. While we were all occupied with this, all hell broke loose. People were everywhere in Lainey's house, even in her dad's bedroom. He had these double doors that opened up to a Juliette balcony overlooking the formal living room, which created a way for a super tall person to reach the vaulted ceiling. One of those super tall people we didn't know thought it would be funny to stick

Lainey's entire elementary school sticker collection to the ceiling. When we finally got Jess out of the bathroom, the phone rang, and we knew it was Lainey's mom calling to check up on her. So she turned off the music and told everyone to shut up, and they did, all two hundred fifty of them. She answered the phone, but then the two hundred fifty people started talking again, and she started "Shhh-ing" them, and then her mom caught on that something was up. As if the night couldn't get any crazier, her mom called the cops. The cops showed up at just about the same time as her mom. I wasn't sure who was scarier, but everyone took off except the original eight. I didn't say a word and just started cleaning up along with everyone else. Lainey's mom was so pissed and started throwing red solo cups into a giant black garbage bag, and because Lainey had one too many shots of Peppermint Schnapps, she started grabbing the cups out of her mom's hand and said, "No, I want to save these for my next party!" Well, that did it. Her mom lost it and started screaming at her in Japanese. I couldn't understand a word of it, but we all knew it wasn't good, and she hadn't even seen the Hello Kitty mosaic on the ceiling yet.

"Peppermint Schnapps, really?" I said.

"No, I'm just kidding. Ava scored us some beer! Come on, it'll be fun!" she said and busted out our dance move to Salt-N-Pepa's "Push It," which consisted of planting your feet hip-width apart and swatting the air side to side while moving your hips in the same direction, trying to go lower and lower each time until you were squatting on the ground, and then repeating the move back up. Whenever this song came on, it was mandatory for us to drop everything and do the dance, and everyone else lucky enough to be in our presence would be forced to watch.

I stopped her mid squat. "Lainey, fine, I'll go," I said, not in the mood to "Push It" just yet.

"Yaaaaaayyyyyyy!" she said and squashed me and all of my cheerleading paraphernalia in a bear hug. She waved to Anna and Jess, who were still standing on the track talking. I'd totally lost track of Collin and Dan in all of my humiliation. I scanned the stands, but I didn't see them. Anna and Jess walked toward us.

"That was *some* show," Anna said.

"Ugh! It was so humiliating! I loathe the school band," I said, which was an enormous understatement.

"Well, you looked cute!" Jess said, trying to make me feel better. It actually did help a little because Jess was adorable with her straight blond bob, freckled nose, huge blue eyes, and her signature fifteen-minute eyelashes, as she called them. It took her fifteen minutes to put on mascara because she used three coats and had to wait five minutes between applications and after the final coat to avoid smudging them.

"Thanks. Okay, can we go now? I really just need to get the heck out of here."

"Yeeeesssss! Let's go. Time to *PAR-TAY*!" Lainey said.

"I'll meet you guys there, I have to change first," I said and trotted off to the locker room before I had to talk to anyone else.

When I get to my car, I discovered where Collin and Dan had been hiding. They were both leaned up against the trunk of my car.

"Duuuuude! Finally!" Dan said. "What took you so long? I'm starving!"

"Dude!" Collin said and smacked Dan in the arm.

"Sorry, I had to change out of my uniform. I didn't know you would be waiting for me. I thought you already left since I didn't see you after the game," I said, my insides flipping upside-down. I was so excited to see Collin, I'd thought for sure he wouldn't have wanted to anything to do with me after that little episode.

"Yeah, we decided to go smoke a bowl after half time. This is as far as we got," Collin said, laughing, his green eyes looking hazy.

"You smoked it by my car?"

"Nope, we hot boxed it in my mom's Honda Accord!" Dan said, and he and Collin started cracking up.

"Honda Accord, chanda achord, chanda achord, that sounds funny!" Collin said with a straight face, making a chopping motion with his hand like he was the president giving a speech, which led to more fits of laughter. "Wait! You have to come with us! Grub sesh at Dan's!"

"Um, I kind of told Lainey that I would go to her house after the game, but you can come. She won't care," I said, hoping that was true, not sure if she was set on a girl's only party.

"No, I want to spend time alone with you. I waited all this time, and now you don't want to come with me?" Collin said, grabbing my arms to look me straight in the face.

"Uh, no, I mean, yes. I do want to come with you. It's just...."

"She won't care, you said so yourself."

"Well, no, not exactly."

"Come on, Lindsay, don't leave me hangin'. I thought you loved me."

"I do. Okay, I'll go with you, but I need to call her when we get to Dan's," I said. I couldn't believe I was blowing off Lainey again.

"Sa-weet! Let's go. Grub sesh!" he said.

"I'll follow you," I said, putting my pom poms in the trunk and getting in my car.

twenty-nine

I didn't know where Dan's house was, so this was probably one of the worst ideas I'd ever had. I had this pit in the bottom of my stomach, but I ignored it. I really loved Collin and wanted to be with him, and he had waited for me. Hopefully, Lainey would understand. She had been such a great friend to me, the first friend I'd had when I moved here. I was starting to miss her. I didn't understand why Collin never wanted to hang out with her. Maybe they were too similar—they both liked being in control and being the center of attention. I guessed you couldn't have two people like that in the same group.

We were driving toward Lainey's neighborhood, which was interesting. Dan lived in the next development over. Collin pulled up in front of what I was assuming was Dan's house since there was a Honda Accord parked in the driveway. There was no room behind him, so I make a U-turn and parked across the street. I was trying to make a mental image of how I'd gotten here so I would know how to leave later.

I walked to Collin's car and waited for him to get out. Dan was already in the house. Collin was in a better mood when he got out the car and gave me a hug. He grabbed my hand to lead me up the stone pathway to the front door. He didn't knock but walked right in, yelling, "Grub sesh!" to no one in particular.

Dan's parents were rich, pack-rat hippies that lived in a mid-century modern Eichler house, high in the hills of San Mateo. Every square inch was covered with artifacts from their travels to Africa or Bali. Dan was a surfer pothead that was stoned every day. His parents didn't seem to want to stifle him with rules. I supposed he needed a break from all the Buddha statues and tribal masks, as I would later find out his room consisted of carpet that had never been vacuumed, a mattress on the floor, and one charcoal sketch of a naked woman taped to the top of the wall near the ceiling.

"Grub sesh!" I heard Dan call from the kitchen. We walked in and saw Dan pulling a large casserole dish out of the fridge.

"My mom made lasagna! Sa-weet!" he said.

"Where is your mom?" I asked.

"She's just left on a business trip," he said and put the lasagna in the oven. "We have twenty minutes, just enough time to smoke another bowl."

He and Collin sat at the table and started stuffing pot into a bong like this was a normal first course to a meal. I sat down next to them. They each took a hit and then offered it to me. I took it and figured nothing had happened last time, so it probably wouldn't do anything this time. Plus, I didn't have the energy to argue.

It smelled disgusting, like dirty, wet, moldy socks. I held the lighter to the bowl like they had and sucked in through the mouthpiece, the water bubbling inside. I was able to hold my breath without coughing this time. I guessed the water made it easier. I finally let it out, and they started cheering for me.

Oh my gosh, I had totally forgotten that I needed to call Lainey. I jumped up.

"Dan, can I use your phone?"

"Be my guest," he said and motioned to the phone hanging on the wall in the kitchen.

I ran over, picked up the phone, and dialed her number. It rang for what seemed like forever before she finally answered.

"Hello?" Lainey said.

"Lainey, I ran into Collin in the parking lot, and he invited me to Dan's. I'm not going to be able to come over."

"What? Lindsay, seriously?"

"I know, I'm sorry," I said. I wanted to tell her that he'd seemed so angry, and I had been a little scared to say no to him, but I couldn't say all that with him sitting right there.

"If my mom asks, I was at your house, okay?" Wow, now I was getting my friends to lie for me. That was an all-time low.

I saw smoke coming out of the oven out of the corner of my eye.

"Fine, yeah, okay, but you owe me," she said.

The smoke alarm went off. Dan and Collin scrambled to the oven. Dan ran around yelling, "Mitts, I need my mitts!" and Collin was flinging a towel at the smoke alarm. For some reason, I started laughing. They looked ridiculous, like they were in some cheesy sitcom or something.

"Is everything okay? Are you high?" I heard Lainey's voice and realized that I'd dropped the phone and it was dangling. I looked at it and then hung it up. Ooops! I guessed I was high.

When Dan and Collin finally figured out how to get the lasagna out of the oven, we discovered that Dan left on the Post-It note with his mom's reheating instructions. The lasagna wasn't burned—and thank God, because I was so hungry by then that I could have gnawed off my own arm.

thirty

Saturday Morning

I walked into the bathroom and paused to look at myself in the mirror. I looked the same as I always did—same long, curly brown hair, same thick brown eyebrows, same faintly freckled face, and same dimple in my chin. But I felt different. I had lied to my mom about where I had been and who I had been with the night before. I felt ugly on the inside. I still had on mascara, and it was smudged under my eyes. I'd been too tired to take it off when I'd gotten home at 2 a.m. I had been too tired to deal with the lecture my mom had given me. Too tired to deal with her accusations. Yes, my hair did smell like smoke. Yes, I was two hours late. Yes, I'd smoked pot. Yes, I was hanging around people I shouldn't have been hanging out with. Yes, I didn't call her to tell her where I was. Yes, I'd made her worry. I'd had all the answers to her questions in my head as I'd sat there and listened to her with my arms crossed, head tilted down, looking down at the cream-colored carpet, but I had been too tired to talk. Unfortunately for me, she had been wide-awake.

There was no way that I was going to tell her what actually happened. I didn't even want to think about it myself. I didn't want to tell her that I'd spent the evening with Collin at his friend Dan's house sitting on the floor of an empty room getting high. I figured Collin was friends with Dan because Dan could score pot for him. Collin didn't smoke pot every day, just occasionally on the weekends. The main reason was that he couldn't afford it, otherwise he probably would have. I would never pay for pot, and if I had to, I wouldn't be smoking it.

What the hell? What was wrong with me? What had happened? I used to care so much about doing the right thing. Now it seemed like I didn't care about anything. Maybe I should have told my mom what had happened. I should have told her how everyone had been sitting around laughing about nothing one minute, and the next minute, Dan had been passed out and I had been arguing with Collin about having to leave because I was going to be late for curfew. At first, he was sweet, saying how he didn't want me to go. He had been hugging me and trying to make out with me, but when I'd pulled away, he'd gotten angry....

"Come on, Lindsay. She won't care if you're a few minutes late," he said.

"It's already twelve-fifteen, and it's gonna take me twenty minutes to get home. She's already gonna be pissed," I said and kneeled to start the standing process. I was midway between kneeling and standing when I felt Collin's hand grip my wrist to yank me down. This knocked me off balance, and I came crashing down on my elbow, hitting my head against the wall.

"You can't go!" he yelled.

"OOOOOWWWWWW!" I hugged my elbow into my chest and rubbed the back of my head. "Collin! What the hell?"

"You care more about your mom than you care about me."

"What? No, I just don't want to be grounded," I said.

"She's trying to split us up, can't you see that? I'm the only one who really cares about you," Collin said and pulled a pack of Marlboro Reds out of his back pocket.

"I know, but if I don't leave, she won't let me see you at all."

"What?" Collin said as he brought a cigarette to his lips. Collin couldn't multitask when he was stoned. He was squinting at the end of the cigarette, trying to get the flame at the end of his lighter to meet the end of his cigarette. His hand-eye coordination was not good in that moment. Realizing this was my chance to make a run for it, I got up and went out the door of Dan's room and down the long narrow hallway that opened up to the large open living and dining room. I could hear Collin stumbling and yelling my name behind me. I passed through the living room and out the front door. I could see my little metallic brown Honda Prelude parked on the street. I was almost there. Collin was now stumbling down the front step, holding the non-lit cigarette in one hand and the lighter in the other. I hadn't locked my car door, so I was able to get in and lock the door before he stumbled to my window.

Where were my keys? I dug through my backpack trying to find the ball of key chains with my car key and house key. He was now banging on my window with flat open palms, shouting my name. I saw a front porch light turn on. I found the wad of key chains and started my car with a shaky hand.

"I'm sorry, I have to go," I yelled to Collin through the window. I was pretty sure he called me a bitch, but I didn't stick around to make sure. I was still shaking. I couldn't make it home like that. When I reached the onramp, I decided to pull over at a gas station to collect myself before I got on the freeway. I started taking deep breaths, but that only made me start crying. The next thing I knew, I was awakened by Axl Rose squealing "Welcome to the Jungle." I must have dozed off. Holy crap! It was 1:30 a.m.! I started driving again, knowing my mom was going to kill me. I rolled down all the windows and blasted the radio to wake up. I pulled up to my house at 1:57 a.m. I held my key chains in one hand and the house key in another to not make any noise while I unlocked the door, but it didn't matter. My mom was sitting on the sofa facing the front door.

"Sit down," she said.

I sat down and assumed the crossed-arm, head-down, hearing-a-lecture position. All of the questions I didn't want to answer were building up like bricks in my head, making it feel heavy.

"Do you have anything to say for yourself?"

"I was at Lainey's, and we were watching a movie, and I fell asleep," I lied.

"Arggghhh! I am so disappointed in you! You had me worried sick! Just go to your room."

I went straight up the stairs to my room. I was too tired to even slam a door like a regular teenager. I just closed it, took off my shoes, and climbed into bed fully clothed.

Now, as I was examining my face in the mirror the next morning, I placed my hands on either side of the bathroom sink and leaned in to get a closer look. I wished I had washed my face the night before. I wished I could wash away the whole night. I wished I could wash away the lies that I'd told. But I couldn't, and now they were a part of me.

I turned on the cold water and splashed it on my face.

thirty-one

My mom was making me go to a shrink. I did *not* want to go. It was something weirdos did, and I was trying so hard not to be a weirdo. When I'd gotten those detentions, she had already been planning on making me go, but now that I had missed curfew, she threatened to ground me if I didn't. So there I was, driving myself to Burlingame after school to meet with this guy. Yeah, a guy—how was I supposed to share all of my innermost secrets with some old dude?

I turned on to Burlingame Avenue from the El Camino. The street was lined with trees on either side that curved in, making a tree tunnel. It was peaceful looking, but I felt anything but peace inside of my brain. I got lucky and found a parking spot a few doors down. I didn't want people to see me going in there. I'd be the pariah again, the freak with mental problems going to "therapy." I dug through my backpack to find the paper where my mom had scribbled the name and address: *Dr. Ross, 303 Burlingame Ave., suite 100.* Great, I was here. I had kind of been hoping I would have gotten lost and missed the appointment, but there I was on time and everything.

I got out of my car, scanning the street to make sure I didn't see anyone I knew. I walked as fast as I could without running to get to the door. I turned the knob, but it was heavy, so I had to use my shoulder to open it. It was an old brick building on the outside, but inside it was like a modern Zen palace. Soft New Age music played and a fountain made of smooth black stones gurgled in the corner. There was no receptionist, only a sign that said, *Please take a seat.* There was no one else in the room, so all of the chairs were empty.

I took a seat as far away from the door as possible, next to an end table topped with a stack of magazines. I picked up the top one, *Psychology Today,* and held it in front of my face in case someone should have happened to walk in and saw me—which was totally ridiculous, because if they came in here, they were probably going to see a shrink, too. Just then, the door to suite 100 opened, and a kid from my school walked out. Thank God I'd picked up the magazine, holy crap, that had been a close one. The kid left, and I put the magazine back down on the table. A tall man with longish gray hair and tortoiseshell glasses peeked out of the doorframe.

"Lindsay?" he said. "Come on in." His voice reminded me of a late-night radio DJ, masculine but calm.

I stood up and followed him into his office. It wasn't as Zen as the lobby, but it was still relaxing in a cozy-book-corner kind of way. There were bookshelves lining two of the walls that were jam packed with books. A giant sofa covered in worn leather sat under the window, and its matching chair floated at an angle in the middle of the room. Between them was a low coffee table with a plant in what looked like a homemade ceramic pot, and beside that a box of tissues. Oh no, I would not be needing those. I had no plans of spilling my guts to this stranger who was giving off a laidback, cool-guy kind of vibe. It wasn't surfer-ish, exactly, but more of a jazz pianist vibe, not at all what I'd pictured a therapist to be like. I wondered if he moonlighted in the evenings with a band.

I zoned out and pictured him playing when he startled me by speaking.

"Have a seat," he said and gestured toward the sofa.

I sat on the sofa and noticed there were three large black file cabinets on the wall next to the door. He walked over to one of them, opened a drawer, and pulled out a file. Wow, there must have been a lot of messed up people for him to have that many files.

"Hello, Lindsay. I'm Dr. Ross. It's nice to finally meet you. Your mother has told me wonderful things about you," he said, opening the file and clicking his pen.

What? My mom's been here? And she's been talking about me *with* him? *If I'm so wonderful, what in the hell am I doing here?* I wanted to scream my thoughts out loud, but I just smiled and said, "Thank you, it's nice to meet you, too." Like I was a robot.

"I want you to know that whatever you say here is confidential. I am legally not allowed to repeat it to anyone, unless of course you are a threat to yourself or others, I am legally obligated to report it. It's called the doctor-patient confidentiality agreement. Do you understand?" he said, looking me straight in the eye. Well, he had nothing to worry about because I wouldn't be sharing anything.

"Yes," I said, hoping he continued with the yes/no questions so I wouldn't have to expand on anything.

"So, I see you are in high school. A senior, correct?"

"Yes," I said. *So far, so good.*

"What classes are you taking?" he said.

Great, now I had to talk in complete sentences. "English, government, physics—you know, the usual."

"Physics, huh? How's that going?"

"Great."

"That's nice to hear. How about extra-curricular activities—are you involved in any of those?" he said.

Ugh, another sentence. "Yes. I'm on the pom pom squad."

"Oh, great! That must be fun."

"Yep."

"That's wonderful."

"Yes, everything is great," I said, hoping he would just say, *Okay, great, nothing to talk about then. Thanks for coming in. Tell your mom I said hi.*

"You know, Lindsay, you don't have to talk if you don't want to. I'm not here to force you to tell me your problems. I get paid either way, but just know that if there is something bugging you, I'm here to listen," he said.

Whoa, I had not expected that.

"Do you like music?"

"Yes."

"I thought it might be nice to listen to some if we're just going to be sitting here for the next hour," he said and got up and walked over to the file cabinets again. He popped a cassette into a small boombox sitting on top of them. "Now, they probably don't play this on MTV, but I think you'll like it."

A classical, fast-paced song with a lot of violins came on. I recognized it as Mozart, but I didn't know the name of it. I never listened to classical music at home. My mom was really into music from the fifties and sixties. She liked girl groups, the Supremes and stuff like that. My grandparents were into big band music, so that was really as far back as it went. The only time I'd listened to classical music was in my Art in Our Lives class.

He sat back down and was quiet for a minute, then said, "So, what do think?"

"I like it. It's Mozart, right?" I said. I figured I could play along with this. At least it kept me from talking about personal stuff.

"Yes! That's right! Do you listen to classical music?"

"No, I just heard it before in a class at school."

"Oh, really? What class?"

"It's called Art in Our Lives. We study art and music of different time periods. We started with jazz and are moving back in time. We just finished the Classical period. We're moving back to the Baroque period now."

"Oh. That's wonderful! I'll have to play you some Bach next time," he said.

Next time? There's going to be a next time? I thought this was it. Ugh! I can't go through this again. I was trying to stay calm, but then my eyes welled up and betrayed me.

"I see that you are having some emotions right now. Do you want to talk about it?"

"No, it's just that I thought this was it. I didn't think I would be coming back here," I said and released the tears I had been holding back.

He nudged the tissue box toward me. I took a tissue and cried for the next few minutes while he sat there and watched me. Finally, I was able to form words again.

"I don't have time for this. I have homework, and cheerleading, and work, and a boyfriend," I blurted out.

"I see. You have all of these responsibilities, and you don't feel like you can fit in one more thing," he said.

"Yes, exactly! It's too much!" I said.

"You're feeling overwhelmed," he said.

Boy, this guy was good, he was basically repeating what I said back to me in different words, but somehow it made more sense when he said it.

"Yeah," I said, staring down at a lock of my hair. I hadn't even realized I was fiddling with it. Now I was looking at it, focusing on the split ends. I couldn't remember the last time I got my hair cut, it was so long ago. I was overwhelmed, but there was nothing I could do about it short of quitting everything, and obviously that was not an option. I worked so hard for all of this, and now it was eating me alive. My mom had to know about all of the stress I'd been under, but then she'd gone and decided to add one more thing to my freakin' to-do list. I mean, seriously, was she trying to make me crazy? Didn't she remember the last time this happened, when we'd left Grass Valley to come to the Silicon Valley? When I'd started getting those massive headaches, and she'd sent me to live with my grandparents? This actually made me pretty happy. I'd loved being with my grandparents. I kind of wished I still lived with them. They didn't bug me about curfews and tardies and shrinks.

A faint bell rang.

"Our time's up. It was nice meeting you, Lindsay. I'll see you next week," Dr. Ross said.

I took another tissue and dried my eyes. "Okay," I said, unsure I wanted to come back, but there was no point arguing about it now.

thirty-two

I got in my car, but I didn't want to go home. I didn't want to get the third degree on how my appointment with the shrink had gone. I started the engine, still undecided on where I was going to go. I backed out of the space and drove down the tree-tunneled street. It came to an end, and I could only go left or right. I decided to go left, the opposite direction of my house. This road wound back around and turned into Crystal Springs Road, which led to Hillsborough, where Collin's dad's house was.

I kept driving. I was trying to remember which way to go. It felt like we'd kept turning right, so I did that, and then I saw it, the long, hidden driveway. I stopped and sat there for a minute. I hadn't seen Collin since I'd run out on him at Dan's house. He hadn't been at school today. I wondered if he was okay. Was he going to be mad at me? He probably wouldn't even remember what happened, he was so out of it. What if Collin wasn't there? What if his dad was outside? Now I was just being ridiculous. He wasn't exactly the gardening type, and I was pretty sure he had other people to take care of the yard and wash his car for him. I'd never know unless I drove up there.

My car was a stick shift, so I drove up as slowly as I could without stalling. I got to the top and saw that Collin's VW was there and the garage door was closed. His dad may or may not have been home. It was only 4:30—he could have still been at work. It was a chance I needed to take.

I got out of my car and tried not to slam the door. I walked up the front steps and knocked on the door. I flipped my hair back behind my shoulders and fiddled with my bangs to make sure they were presentable. Lip gloss! I could have really used some lip gloss. I swung my backpack around to unzip the front pocket. I didn't carry a purse on school days, and I knew I looked like a dork with my backpack, but I needed someplace to put my keys and everything.

The door opened, and Collin popped his head out while my hand dug into my backpack. The lip gloss would have to wait.

"Hey, Lindsay, what's up?" he said like nothing happened.

"Hey, um, nothing. I was just worried about you since you weren't at school today, and I haven't talked to you since Dan's house. I thought maybe you were sick or mad at me," I said.

"Oh, yeah. Nah, I just didn't feel like going to school today. Plus, my dad's out of town, so no one to hassle me about it."

"Can I come in, or do you just want to sit out here and talk?" I said. I really did want to talk about what happened the other night. I knew I should have been mad at him for how he'd treated me, but somehow I couldn't muster up the nerve to say anything. Maybe it was my fault. Maybe I wasn't clear earlier that night. I mean, I didn't tell him that I had to leave at a certain time, and that made him angry. I didn't always say what I was feeling. I didn't want to make people angry. I wanted them to like me.

"Oh yeah, sorry," Collin said. He reached for my hand, pulled me in, and closed the door. I set my backpack down next to the door and just stood there looking at him, not really sure what to do with myself or what to say. I wasn't really sure why I'd driven myself here. I wasn't really sure about anything right then. I thought in the back of my head that I shouldn't be here. I should have gone straight home. I should walk away now and never speak to Collin again after what happened at Dan's house last weekend. But I had this aching feeling in my chest—a feeling that he needed help, and I was the one to help him.

I felt sweat beading up on my temples and upper lip. Collin pulled me in for a hug, and the floor dropped below us. We were floating in space. Everything went dark, and there was no sunlight, but it was comfortable here in this place. A warm musky air swirled around us. His arms felt strong around me; they were the only thing holding me up. We didn't talk. We didn't need to say anything.

thirty-three

I saw red-and-blue flashing lights in my rear-view mirror. Crap! It was a cop on a motorcycle. Maybe he was after someone else. I slowed down and pulled over to the side. He followed me. Nope, he wasn't after someone else. I came to a stop, wracking my brain on why I was being pulled over. I honestly couldn't even remember how I'd gotten here, my mind was totally distracted thinking about Collin, the shrink, and what I was going to tell my mom about where I'd been for the past four hours.

The cop tapped on my window, startling me. He motioned for me to roll down my window.

"Do you have any idea how fast you were going?" he said, peeling off his sunglasses to reveal his blue-gray eyes and bushy furrowed brow.

"Um, thirty-five?" I said, which I knew was wrong. I didn't even know what the speed limit was.

"I clocked you at fifty. This is a twenty-five mile per hour zone."

"Oh my gosh! I am so sorry," I said and felt my nose prickle and eyes water. I was sorry, I didn't mean to speed, and now I had to explain this to my mom. This hole I was digging for myself was getting so big. I didn't feel like I could get myself out.

"License and registration," he said, writing on a metal clipboard.

Oh God! Did I have that? I fumbled with the glove box handle and yanked it down hard to get it to open. It was jammed full with stuff. I searched for the envelope my stepdad had told me to keep in there. I found it and handed him the whole thing. Then I dug through my backpack to find my wallet. My hands were shaking and the tears were flowing. The cop cocked his head to the side and sighed. I could tell he was getting impatient, which made me even more nervous. I finally pulled my license out of its little plastic window and handed that over.

He took it and walked back to his motorcycle, completely unsympathetic to my tears. Oh my God! Was he calling for backup? I could just picture it—my mom in her bathrobe having to come bail me out of jail. Would it be jail? I wouldn't turn eighteen until January. But I heard all the time about kids who got tried as adults. Holy crap! But jail probably would be better than whatever punishment my mom could dish out.

This wasn't even my first offense. I'd gotten a ticket about a year before when I first got my license. I'd been turning right and didn't come to a complete stop because I'd wanted to go before all the cars started coming by. I had gone out to pick up ice cream for the family in my stepdad's black convertible Mustang, and I forgot my license, so that ticket was a doozy! The cop had been so mean to me. She was a female and seemed to be trying to prove a point that she could be as big of a jerk as any man. She'd actually said to me, "You can go ahead and turn off the engine and radio because we're going to be here a while." And then, as if that wasn't bad enough, she'd followed it with, "This is a pretty nice car for a girl your age to be driving."

The cop handed my license and the envelope with my registration back to me. Then he did some more scribbling on his clipboard and ripped off a piece of paper, which he handed to me as well.

"Slow down," he said and walked away.

I was stunned. Not knowing what to do, I just sat there. I saw him pull away, make a U-turn, and drive off out of my vision. I looked at the paper in my hand. It was a speeding ticket. I didn't freak out right away until I noticed it was for three hundred dollars. Holy crap! How was I going to explain this? How was I going to pay for this? I had a job, but it was only part time. It would take me two months to come up with this. They were going to haul me away for sure. The tears hadn't worked on the police officer. I hoped they'd work on my mom.

Well, I'm not going to say that my mom wasn't mad at me, but it wasn't as bad as I thought, and the ticket distracted her from asking about the shrink.

"Why were you speeding?"

"I didn't realize I was speeding. I didn't see any signs."

"I think you can fight this in traffic court. Did you argue with the police officer?"

"No."

"Did you say anything at all?"

"No, well, I did start crying and said I was sorry."

"Hmmm, there's a chance he won't show up if he doesn't remember you. If he doesn't show up, they drop the case."

"What happens if he does show up?"

"They will either make you pay the fine or let you go to traffic school. It's worth a shot."

"Okay, that's okay, I guess. I hope he doesn't show up."

"Yeah, me too," she said.

thirty-four

After I got the speeding ticket, my mom put me on partial restriction. I was only allowed to go out on the weekends, which was fine because football season was over, and basketball season was about to start, so pom pom practices were going a little longer, and I still had tons of homework. I went over to Collin's every weekend. My court date was coming up. We had been able to schedule it for a minimum day so that I didn't have to miss school and my mom could meet me there on her lunch break. Since school got out at 12:15 and my appointment was at 2, I figured I had time to go to Collin's for lunch.

"Collin, I have to go. I have court. If I am late my mom will literally kill me. It's already one-thirty," I said.

"Come on, just a few more minutes. I need you to stay with me. Plus, it only takes twenty minutes to get there," he said and pulled me in for another kiss. He knew what to say to get me to give in. Sometimes I was too nice. No, I was always too nice. I always gave in to what other people wanted.

Well, there was that one time in the summer between sixth and seventh grade when I'd stood up for myself against Maeve, but that had been a total disaster. I'd lost my best friend and spent most of junior high as a loner/loser.

"Fine. Just a few more minutes, but then I really have to go," I said and nuzzled my cheek into his shoulder for a hug. Normally, I would have been swept away and lost track of time, but I was too nervous about my court appointment. If the cop showed up, I could still have to pay. I prayed he didn't show up...*Please don't show up, please don't show up, please don't show up.*

I looked at the clock on the microwave. It said 1:40. "Is that clock right?"

"Yeah, my dad is totally anal about stuff like that."

"Oh my God, I need to go," I said and jumped up. I wasn't giving Collin a chance to stall anymore. I just ran straight out the front door. "Love you," I called from the driveway, not looking back. I couldn't have him using his powers on me. I heard him calling my name, but I just got in my car and locked the door.

As I drove, I envisioned getting pulled over for speeding again—that would have been just my luck. Finally, I saw the courthouse. The parking lot was jam packed with cars. I drove around three times to find a spot. Sweat beads formed on my upper lip. The clock on my car said 2:05. Crap! I got out, slammed the door, and ran to the entrance and into the lobby.

Before I went in, I wiped the sweat off my face, smoothed out my skirt, and flipped my hair behind my shoulders. Okay, I was ready. I opened the door. The courtroom was about halfway filled with people. Everyone turned to look at who was coming in, which meant everyone was now looking at me. I saw my mom glaring at me from an aisle seat about four rows back from the judge. I looked down at the floor to avoid eye contact and walked as fast and as quietly as I could to take the empty seat next to my mom.

"Where the hell have you been?" she said in an angry whisper.

Where the hell *had* I been? I blurted out in a loud whisper the first thing that came to my mind: "I had to make Collin lunch." Wow, that was lame.

My mom gave me a death stare.

"Citation 45679," the judge called out.

"That's you," my mom said and handed me my ticket. She'd taken it from me when I'd first gotten it because she hadn't trusted me not to lose it. She had probably been right not to trust me, I'd been so preoccupied lately that there was a greater than fifty percent chance that I would have lost the stupid thing.

I got up and walked down the aisle and stood in front of the judge.

"Let's see. This citation was issued by Officer Martin, and he is not here. This is your lucky day, young lady." She scribbled something on a piece of paper and outstretched her arm with it in her hand in my direction. "Case dismissed. Take this to the clerk to check out."

Whoa, I was so stunned not only at how fast that happened but at my amazing luck that I practically tripped over my own feet to take the paper and did this weird hop-step thing. I heard snickering from the back of the room and saw my mom with her face in her hand shaking her head. I had no idea where the clerk was, so I thanked the judge and walked out of the room. My mom followed; I could hear her heels clicking on the industrial tiles.

"Wow, Lindsay! I cannot believe how lucky you are because I was going to kill you if you showed up any later," my mom said and stared at me with her mouth open.

"I know. I can't believe it either! Where's the clerk?" I said and looked away from her visual disapproval.

"Upstairs, I think. Let's get this over with quick in case good ol' Officer Martin decides to show up," my mom said, and for once we were in complete agreement.

thirty-five

"I missed you last week," Dr. Ross said, opening my file and clicking his pen.

I took this as more of a rhetorical statement, something adults used when they were disappointed in you but didn't want to come out and say it. Was I supposed to say something? I had nothing to say. I found it hard to believe he could have actually missed me after meeting me one time for an hour. I didn't show up for our appointment the week before because I'd had a paper due the next day. I mean, yes, I could have worked on it over the weekend, but I'd needed a break.

I needed a break from school. I needed a break from my mom. I needed a break from reality. Things were just getting a little too real for me. Maybe that was why I wanted to be with Collin so much. When I was with him, I felt like I was in a different world. It was a world where rules didn't exist. I was so tired of following the rules. I guessed what I really needed was a break from the rules. Collin just did whatever he wanted to do, whenever he wanted to do it.

All I knew was that I really didn't want to be here in this office, on this leather sofa, talking about my problems with a stranger.

"What happened?" he finally asked, breaking the silent standoff we had going.

I wanted to say that I just hadn't wanted to be here so I'd been avoiding him, but I thought that might buy me more time with this guy.

"I had a paper due," I said.

"Oh, well, that's understandable. You mentioned last time that you had a lot to do. Do you feel like you are managing your time better now?"

"Yes," I said. *Can I go now? I'm okay, nothing to report.*

"That's great. You were able to get your work done and are feeling less overwhelmed," he said. There he went again with the psychiatrist mind games, repeating what I said to get me to say more. I was on to him. I'd taken an intro to psych class the year before. We'd learned about Freud and how everything was our mother's fault, which I didn't totally agree with. Dads could really mess you up, too. Like the time Bill Warner squashed Bill Warner, Jr., with his backpack.

I'd managed to salvage my grade and not get an "F" for killing my egg baby because I'd written an awesome paper about how important it was to have two responsible parents, and my teacher had totally bought it. I didn't even have to add anything about my real dad. I mean, if you looked up "terrible parent" in the dictionary, my real dad's picture would have been right there with Collin's dad.

I remembered one time sitting in the cab of my dad's Ford pick-up truck on the brown vinyl bench seat trying to breathe through the stale cigarette smell. There was a scary man sitting behind the steering wheel with jet black hair and a mustache and dark tanned skin from years of working outdoors. My bladder was uncomfortably full, so he pulled over. I didn't want to pee on the side of the road. I couldn't hold it any longer. My pants became warm, and my eyes welled up with tears. I felt him looking at me. I knew the yelling would start soon.

"Goddammit!" he yelled. He kept yelling, but I stopped listening and stared at the grooves in the vinyl and traced the pattern with my fingernails.

"So what was your paper about?" Dr. Ross said.

"It was about Mozart," I said.

"Oh, yes, that's right. You said you were studying the Classical period. Would you like to hear some more music?"

"Sure," I said. *Why not?* It would help pass the time.

He walked over to the boombox sitting on the file cabinet and rifled through his cassette collection.

"Ah, here it is," he said and popped the cassette into the boombox. The music started playing, and he stood there for a moment, pantomiming a music conductor. "Do you recognize this one?"

"Is it Beethoven?" I guessed. My teacher just played this for us in class the other day.

"Yes, very good. It's Beethoven's Fifth Symphony, probably one of the most popular pieces," he said and went back to his chair, picked up my file, and sat down.

I was kind of hoping he would have forgotten about that stupid file, but no such luck.

Da Da da Da! Beethoven seemed to be mocking me. We sat without speaking for a minute, listening to the strings and the horns.

"So, you don't want to talk about life at school right now. Tell me about what life was like for you when you were a kid, well, a younger kid. I see that your birthday is in January, and you'll be eighteen, so you're almost an adult," he said, smiling, like he was trying to break the ice and get on my good side. Like we were sharing some inside joke. Like he was the cool, understanding guy in some afterschool special on TV.

I really didn't want to talk about anything, but I figured it wouldn't hurt to throw this guy a bone. I did feel bad for him. Maybe if I said something, he'd report back to my mom that I was fine, and I could stop coming here.

"Ummm, well, I was born in Santa Clara, but my dad worked for Cal Trans, you know, those guys you see working on the side of the road, that was him, and we moved a lot. I don't remember it, my mom told me," I said, which was true. I really didn't remember that time in my life.

"Oh, that's interesting. Do you know where you lived?"

"My mom said we moved to Southern California and lived in Redondo Beach for about a year. Then my dad got transferred again, and we moved back to Northern California to Penn Valley."

"Penn Valley, I'm not familiar with that. Where is that exactly?"

"It's in the country. It's the middle of nowhere. Kind of on your way to go to Tahoe," I said and had a flash of memory. "I remember the leaves, they were tiny and sharp and everywhere. There was a huge tree and a sandbox." I felt a surge of anxiety. I couldn't talk anymore. I didn't want to start crying. Why would I cry over this?

"You remember a tree and a sandbox? That's great. Do you remember if they were in your backyard, or was it a park? It sounds like an oak tree," he said, looking me in the eye.

I looked away. I could feel the tears coming on. I took a deep breath and tried to push them back.

"Yes, I remember." Another deep breath. "It was in our yard." My heart was beating faster.

"What else do you remember?" he said, and the music got softer. I took another deep breath.

"I remember it being quiet outside. I remember not wanting to go inside. I remember a large fluffy dog," I said and kept taking deep breaths. The images in my head of the dog and the sandbox had pushed away the tears for now.

"Oh, you remember you had a big fluffy dog. That's wonderful. Do you remember its name or what kind of dog it was?" he said.

"I'm trying to remember. It was one of those dogs that lived in the Alps and rescued people," I said.

"A St. Bernard?" he said.

"Yes, I think so."

"Wow, that is a big fluffy dog."

"Yeah."

"You mentioned it being quiet outside and that you didn't want to go inside. Was it too loud inside?"

"No, I can't remember exactly. I just felt scared about going inside. I can't really explain it."

"I see. Well, that was very productive. I think it will help you to explore your memories. Unfortunately, we are just about out of time for today. Did you have anything else you wanted to add before you go?"

"Annie."

"Annie?"

"The dog's name was Annie."

thirty-six

_____

I was sitting in my English class staring out the windows that lined the classroom on the northern side that faced out to the parking lot. The windows were not at eye level, so instead of seeing parked cars, I saw the tops of the trees. There was a blank piece of white paper on my desk. I was supposed to be writing a poem, but instead I was staring out the windows, thinking about my appointment with Dr. Ross. I had been thinking about it all night. I hadn't slept well. Deep down, I knew why I had been afraid to go into the house. I remembered always wanting to draw on white paper with my crayons. I wasn't sure if I was obsessed with drawing or if that was all I had. Maybe it was my toddler self's way to escape or stay out of the way. Anyway, it was all I could remember, only the white paper and the crayons. I started writing.

Lindsay Trifling
CP English – Per. 1

Mr. Averman
Perfect Paper Houses
A Poem

I like to draw. I draw perfect houses over and over and over and over and over again. A perfect house, was there such a thing? I wanted it to be true, so I drew them. I drew them with flowers in the yard, I drew them with a perfect blue sky, I drew them with a yellow sun in the corner, I drew them with white birds soaring overhead and I drew them with stick figures of smiling families standing next to them. There was always a mom, a dad, a brother, a sister, a dog and a cat. Perfect. The coloring had to be just so. The coloring had to be in the lines. I had to be in the lines. Perfect. I never dared to go out of the lines. Stay in the lines, sit quietly, don't complain, do what you're told. When you step out there will be yelling, when you step out there will be tears, when you step out there will be disappointment, when you step out there will be pain. Do not step out of the lines! I draw my pictures over, and over and over and over and over again. I can make them perfect.

I was so deep in thought that I didn't notice Collin standing in the hall waiting for me when I walked out of class. I was looking at the ground and smacked right into him.

"Hey, Dimples, what's up?" he said and grabbed me by the shoulders.

"Oh my gosh, I'm so sorry. I totally didn't see you," I said.

"Yeah, I noticed. You looked pretty out of it. Maybe this will wake you up," he said and planted a kiss right on my lips that sent a jolt through my body. I pulled back almost on instinct. I really didn't like kissing in public.

"Uh, yep! Now I'm awake," I said.

"Guess what?"

"What?"

"I had to drop physics, and it totally f'ed up my schedule, but we are in the same English class now! I came over here to get Mr. A to sign my admit slip. Isn't that totally fucking awesome!" he said and pulled me in for a bear hug.

"Uh, yeah," I said, but it came out muffled because my face was pressed into his shoulder.

He let me go, adjusted his backpack on his shoulder, and flopped his hair over. I forced a smile, but I actually had mixed feelings about us being in another class together because I thought we would get too distracted. I was having flashbacks to how distracted I had been by him in our algebra class last year, and the thought of having him sitting in the same room as me in English made me cringe a little on the inside.

"I have more good news! I got the tickets to the Grid! I'm totally stoked!" he said and flipped his hair the other way, flashing his super white smile. That was great, I guessed. The Grid was what we called the winter formal. I wondered if Lainey was going and if we could all go together since she had stopped calling me and asking me to come over. I hadn't noticed it at first, but when she stopped looking for me at break and lunch, I knew something was up. I mean, I was spending all of my free time with Collin, but, seriously, we could have still hung out together. It wasn't just Lainey, either, I wasn't really hanging out with any of my friends. Collin and I were always alone or with his friends. I didn't mind hanging out with his friends, they were fun, but he always got mad when I said I wanted to hang out with my friends, so I'd just stopped talking about it. Anyway, I saw the Grid as a good opportunity to get our two friend groups together.

"That's so awesome! Thank you! I can't wait to talk to Lainey to see if she got a date. Oh my God! This is going to be so fun!" I said just as the bell rang. Perfect timing. It didn't give Collin time to come up with an excuse to not hang out with Lainey. Plus, I knew he still had to talk to Mr. A during the break.

"Gotta go! I need to find Lainey. Bye!" I said and gave him a quick kiss on the cheek and ran down the hall. I didn't turn around to wait for him to answer. My plan was to talk to Lainey and then write him a note with our plans for before and after the Grid. I felt like if it was written down, it would be more permanent. I knew she had English right after the break, but I wanted to catch her before she headed over to the English department.

I was weaving between students like a football player heading for the end zone when I saw her.

"Hey, Lainey," I said and stopped to catch my breath.

"Lindsay! Wow, long time no see. How's Collin, and to what do I owe the honor of your presence, m'lady?" she said and curtsied.

"Just finished the unit on Shakespeare, I presume," I said, and we both laughed, which was a good sign. I had been worried she might have been mad at me. "Funny, that's what I wanted to talk to you about. Collin and I are going to the Grid, and I wanted to know if you were going and if we could go together," I said, holding my breath and closing my eyes, praying she would say yes.

"Well, I don't have an actual date just yet, but my cousin Danny said he would go with me, which is totally lame, and I'm not sure I could bear the humiliation of that, buuuuuuut I do love a good party. So, yeah, what the hell!"

"Yay! I am so excited!" I said and pulled her in for a hug and then immediately pushed her back to look at her face. "What about Anna and Jess?"

"Well, as you probably heard, Anna is dating Matt now, but we need to figure out Jess's situation. No worries, though, we'll figure it out."

"What should we do before and after?"

"I think they serve dinner at this thing, so we just meet up there, and then we can have the after party at my house."

"Are you sure? Remember what happened when you had that party last year?"

"Yeah, my mom was so pissed," she said and laughed. "That's why my dad will have to be there, but he's chill. I will just send him up to his room. He won't bother us."

"Okay, awesome. Thank you, Lainey!" I said and hugged her again just as the bell rang for third period.

Dear Collin,

Sorry I ran out on you so fast. I wanted to catch Lainey before third period. We're all set for the Grid. You'll come pick me up, and we'll meet up there. Then Lainey is having the after party at her house. Sound good? I can't wait to go dress shopping. I'm so excited to go with you to the Grid. You are the best boyfriend ever! I mean it! I love spending every minute with you. Even English is exciting now! I can't wait to proof-read with you!

XOXO,

Love, Lindsay

I folded up the note in my usual triangle origami style and put it in the back pocket of my jeans so it would be ready for the hand-off on the way to fourth period English class.

Dear Lindsay,

First of all, that was the sweetest note you have ever written me. I love you sweetie x 1000 more. (Not enough room for all the zeros) You have no idea how great that letter made me feel. Kiss Kiss Hug Hug! XOXO

That's bullshit about being the best boyfriend ever but thank you anyways. Hey Lindsay, lets subtract and multiply and do square roots and the works. Hey and ya better quit wearing those awesome white Guess jeans, I can't take it! Anyway, I can't wait for the Grid either, especially going with you. I love you and you are the best girlfriend I will and have ever had. Stay with me!

I love you! Love, Collin

P.S. – What a mushy fuckin' letter

thirty-seven

Here's the sad recap of the Grid:

On January 6, 1990, Collin picked me up at 18:00 hours:

For thirty minutes, we proceeded with the most awkward photo shoot I've ever had, complete with wisecracks from my stepdad about Collin's shoe selection—sneakers with a suit. Hey, at least he'd been wearing a suit. I fake smiled the whole time because I would rather have climbed under a rock. We made a mad dash for the door just in time to hear my mother yell at me to be home by midnight. I yelled back, "Okay, glass slippers and all."

18:30 hours:

We climbed into the VW. I was careful not to slam my strapless black lace mini dress in the door.

We drove to the Grid location in Burlingame at the Hyatt Hotel near the water.

18:50 hours:

We parked a few blocks away because—*surprise*—Collin brought some pot. We proceeded to smoke said pot and did not notice the undercover police officers parked across the street. So when the police officers approached the vehicle with badges hanging around their necks and pounded on the windows, ordering us out of the vehicle, I almost had a heart attack.

19:00 hours:

I had my hands on the side of Collin's VW and was being frisked in my strapless black lace mini dress while another officer searched the VW. Because Collin did not have a part-time job and was poor, they did not find any more drugs or drug paraphernalia and let us go with a warning.

19:30 hours:

We walked into the hotel, my hair still perfectly coifed despite the frisking. For the next two hours, I retold the story to Lainey, Anna, and Jess, who couldn't believe my hair still looked perfect.

21:30 hours:

We caravanned up to Lainey's house. Lainey sent her dad to his room as promised and loud music played for the next two hours. Somewhere during that time, Collin convinced me to go out to his car to talk. We did not talk but instead steamed up the windows.

23:30 hours:

I went back into Lainey's house to say goodbye and fix my hair, which no longer looked perfect.

24:30 hours:

Collin and I pulled up in front of my house. I spent fifteen minutes saying goodbye to Collin. I did not walk into my house until 24:45 hours, at which time the record would show that I was late.

thirty-eight

That night, I had this weird dream. I used to have the same dream all the time when I was little. What was weird about it was that I was having it again now. I dreamt that I was back in my canopy bed, in my room on Meadows Road in Grass Valley. The canopy was draped in a fabric with tiny pink, yellow, green, and blue flowers that matched the comforter. The comforter reversed to reveal a pink gingham fabric with a white eyelet lace trim. The bed itself was painted white with flecks of beige, which matched my dresser and the oval mirror on the other side of the room. There was a line of yellow flowers with green leaves carved into the headboard, the same kind of flower that was on the comforter. It was far too frilly to be scary, yet I lay there in my bed trembling. Someone else was in the room, but it was so dark. We lived way out in the country, so there were no streetlights. The only light came from a tiny crescent moon thousands of miles away. It was almost pitch black. I could only make out a shadow moving toward my bed. I wanted to scream, but I couldn't make any sound. I wanted to run, but the floor was moving. It was covered with snakes, so all I could do was close my eyes, curl up into a ball, and clutch my Raggedy Ann doll tightly into my chest. I stopped trying to scream, and then I was falling, falling, falling, falling, falling.

I jerked to a stop, awake now in a different room. It was my current room. The comforter still had flowers on it, but they were larger, more sophisticated, and in shades of dusty pink and burgundy. A whitewashed oak sleigh bed had replaced the canopy bed. The light from the street was almost too bright, and I could see the window was cracked open, causing the metal blinds to swing out and then back, tapping the sill on occasion. The jasmine planted beneath my second-floor window filled the room with perfume. Even though the air was warm, I felt a chill. The oversized Paula Abdul concert t-shirt I was wearing as pajamas was soaked through.

I sat up in my bed and looked at the floor. It was still. Yesterday's jeans and sweatshirt lay motionless in front of my closet door, and there wasn't a snake to be found. I placed my feet on the white carpet, relieved that I was here, now, seventeen rather than eight years old. Thinking about being eight years old sent a shiver up my spine. Why? And why was I having that dream again?

I pulled off my soaked t-shirt, reached down, found another t-shirt on the floor, and put that on. I pushed my matted, heavy curls away from my face and took four steps across my small room to search for my keepsake box under my dressing table. I found it tucked behind my old yearbooks. I knelt on the floor and set the box on my lap. What was I looking for? And then I saw it—a small rock with tiny flecks of gold. I held it in my hand. It felt rough. Fool's gold.

I started to remember the day I'd found it on a fourth-grade field trip. I dropped it back into the box, closed the lid, and shoved the box back behind the yearbooks. No, I didn't want to think about that. I stood up and took one leaping step back to my bed and pulled the comforter and its pink flowers over my head. It was over, it was done, and I was never going back there—I didn't need to think about it anymore.

thirty-nine

Dear Lindsay,

Hey! What's up honey pie? (sweetie, cutie or whatever) How was physics? I can't make this note too long because Mrs. Franser is playing stupid Othello and neither Charlotte or I understand this shit. How about you? I can't wait to go skiing this weekend! Did you really have fun before and after the Grid. I sure as hell did. Whenever I spend time like that with you I feel great and have a blast. Anyways, you make me very happy and I hope I make you very happy and I love you very much! Tahoe will be awesome. Yah, we should get buds but not totally necessary. I don't need to be frisked again, well, unless you're doing the frisking. Just being around you is good enough. Yee-Haw!!! Well honey *pie, I must depart from this world and enter the wonderful world of Othello.*

See ya later, I love ya, Collin

Either my mom was easing up on me because I was going to the shrink or because I was about to turn eighteen in two weeks, or she was using reverse psychology. When Collin asked me to go on a ski trip to Tahoe with him for my birthday, I was shocked when she said yes. I thought sure she would have ripped into her "If you're living under my roof, then you follow my rules" speech, but she didn't. I explained to her that we would be staying at Collin's grandma's house in Reno overnight in *separate* rooms, and she didn't even flinch. She said it was okay like I was asking to go out for ice cream or something, like it was no big deal. She had only one condition—I had to make my shrink appointment before I left, no skipping out. Fine. I could do that. I packed the night before, and Collin picked me up from school and loaded all of my stuff into his dad's blazer, which he'd borrowed for the trip. That was another miracle—he and his dad were actually speaking to each other and not in some big fight. After school, Collin took me to the shrink's office and waited outside for me.

"Good afternoon, Lindsay," Dr. Ross greeted me at his office door.

"Hi," I said and sat in my usual spot on the leather sofa.

"So, how's your week been?"

"Great! My mom is letting me go on a ski trip for the weekend with my boyfriend."

"Wow, that *is* great! Are you meeting any friends up there?" he said.

"No, it'll be just us, but we will be staying with his grandma," I said.

"Hmmm," he said.

What did he mean by that, *Hmmm*? We sat without talking for a minute.

"My son is going up with a group of friends, so I thought maybe you were going on the school trip," he finally said. Okay, so he wasn't being judgmental. My mom had been making comments lately that I should try hanging out with my friends more. Collin said his dad had been saying the same thing to him. Stuff like, *There's plenty of fish in the sea* and *You'll have plenty of time to date when you're out of college.* I mean, I did miss my friends sometimes, but the fact was Collin and I were just drawn to each other. We couldn't help it. He was always there for me, picking me up for school in the morning, waiting for me after practice, and then driving me home. It was sweet. Nobody understood us. It was like it was us against the world.

"Oh, that's cool. No, I'm not going on the school trip," I said. I wanted to change the subject, so I blurted out, "I had a dream." *Why did I say that?*

"Oh. Do you want to talk about it?" he said.

Ugh! Not really. I was such an idiot. I couldn't believe I'd brought that up. Now I had to talk about stuff.

"Um, it was weird." Oh boy, here we go.

"Weird, how so? Was it a bad dream?" he said.

"Kind of. It was weird because I used to have it all the time when I was little." I literally could not believe these words were coming out of my mouth. I really did not want to talk about this.

"That's interesting. You used to have a reoccurring dream when you were younger, and now suddenly you're having it again," he said. There he went with the repeating thing again.

"Yeah, I mean, yes," I said and almost continued on about how scared I used to get when I had the dream. I would be paralyzed by fear. I wouldn't be able to move. I would barely be able to breathe. I was afraid of the snakes; they were always surrounding the floor beneath my bed. Why were the snakes coming back? Were they warning me about something? How? Everything was going so great right now. It wasn't like back then. I left all that behind when we'd moved—that life was over. I didn't want to think about it anymore. I didn't want to remember, I just wanted to forget about it and leave it in the past. Why was this coming back to haunt me? I felt my face getting hot and the tears welling up.

Stop it, Lindsay. Don't do this. You're about to go on an awesome trip with your boyfriend. Snap out of it.

Dr. Ross nudged the tissues toward me. I took one, sat back, crossed my arms, and stared at the bookshelf.

"You know, Lindsay, if you're not ready to talk about it, that's okay," he said.

Thank God. No, I definitely wasn't ready to talk about it. I didn't ever want to be ready to talk about it.

"Thanks," I said.

The timer dinged—saved by the bell.

forty

After wiping my eyes and giving my nose a good hard blow in the bathroom of Dr. Ross' office, I was ready to go. I walked up the street to where Collin was parked. The tree tunnel was swaying in gusts of wind that sent a flurry of little leaves fluttering to the ground. Collin was leaning on the Blazer smoking. I had mentioned to him the last time we were together that I really didn't like smoking, and he'd said he was going to cut back.

And, right on cue, as if he was reading my mind, he said, "Last one, I promise." He crushed it out, smiled, and gestured to the door. "Your chariot awaits, m'lady."

I laughed a little harder than I meant to, but it was a relief to not be thinking about the shrink anymore. We hopped in and cranked the tunes, then sang at the top of our lungs and air guitared the solos to Tesla's "Love Song":

"So you think that it's over
That your love has finally reached the end
Anytime you call, night or day
I'll be right there for you when you need a friend, yeah

It's gonna take a little time
Time is sure to mend your broken heart
Don't you worry, pretty darlin'
I know you'll find love again

Yeah, love is all around you
Love is knockin' outside your do-or-or
Waitin' for you is this love made just for two
Keep an open heart and you'll find love again, I know

Love is all around you, yeah
Love is knockin' outside your do-or-or
Waitin' for you is this love made just for two
Keep an open heart and you'll find love again, I know."

It was a four-hour drive to Collin's grandmother's house, so that got us there around 9 p.m., since we stopped for dinner on the way. Everything was going so amazingly, time was flying by, and we were so in-synch with each other—until we got to his grandma's house.

She lived in a one-bedroom apartment, and we were planning to sleep in sleeping bags on the floor of her living room. She was really sweet and made sure we had everything we needed. She helped us move her coffee table so we would have room to roll out our sleeping bags, and then she went to bed.

"Goodnight, Gran," Collin said.

"Goodnight, dear," she called from her door and then closed it.

Collin lay down on his side on top of his sleeping bag with his head propped up on his hand. "Okay, come over here so we can snuggle," Collin said and patted the floor next to him.

"Um, I don't think that's a good idea," I said, standing over him.

"Why?"

"Your grandma is in the next room, and it's not like we can lock the door."

"She won't come out here."

"How do you know? What if she gets thirsty and comes out for a glass of water?"

"She won't."

"What if she hears us?"

"She's practically deaf. She can't hear anything."

"I don't know, it just doesn't feel right."

"Come *on*, Lindsay," he said. I could tell by his tone that he was getting annoyed.

"Remember your mom's house? I was so humiliated."

"That's not going to happen again. You just don't want to be with me."

"That's not true. I love you, but I just don't want to do this right now. I'm tired, and I just want to go to sleep."

"You don't really love me. If you did, you would want to be with me. You know I'm the only one who really cares about you. So get over here, now!" he said and yanked my arm down, catching me off guard so that I fell on top of him while bumping into the coffee table, almost knocking over a vase of fake flowers.

"Owww. Collin, stop it," I said in a loud whisper. "Let me go."

"Fine, be a bitch. I don't care," he said. He shoved me off of him and rolled over to his other side with his back to me.

I wanted to grab my stuff and run out of the apartment, but I couldn't. I had nowhere to go. I decided to not say another word and got in my sleeping bag. I couldn't sleep, and I knew he was awake, too. I wanted to cry, but I was too angry. So far, this had been the worst birthday ever. I turned away from him and shut my eyes and prayed for the morning to come.

I finally fell asleep right before Collin's grandma got up. I heard her puttering around the kitchen and then I smelled coffee. I didn't drink coffee, but I loved the smell of it, and it woke me up. I saw Collin had rolled up his sleeping bag but was not in the room. I heard the toilet flush and then saw him come out of the bathroom.

"Hi, honey. Do you two want some breakfast?" his grandmother said.

"No, that's okay, Gran. We're just going to grab something on the road, we want to hit the slopes early," he said like nothing had happened.

I took this as my cue to roll up my sleeping bag. "Good morning," I said to Collin's grandma and then took my turn in the bathroom. I didn't make eye contact with Collin, I was still so angry with him. I didn't even want to go skiing any more, I just wanted to go home.

We packed up our stuff in silence, said goodbye and thank you to his grandma, and headed out to the car. I still had nothing to say to him. I got in the car, slammed the door, and looked straight ahead. I didn't think he realized I was mad at him at first, but then after a few failed attempts at conversation while he was starting up the engine and turning on the heater, he figured it out.

"Lindsay, are you mad at me?"

"Kind of," I said, still not looking at him.

"About last night?"

"Yeah."

"I'm sorry, it's just I love you so much, and when you don't want to be with me, I get scared. I think you don't love me. I promise it will never happen again."

"I do love you," I said and turned to look at him.

"I know. I'm sorry. Can you give me a kiss now?" he said and put his hands together like he was praying.

"You promise you won't do that again?"

"I promise," he said and smiled that smile where the corners of his eyes wrinkled. His eyes looked even greener than normal.

I knew I should have asked him to take me home, but I didn't. I couldn't resist his smile. I couldn't resist him, period. I let him kiss me. I thought for a minute that we would just sit there kissing in the car forever, but then he stopped.

"I'm hungry. Time for a grub sesh!" he said, and we both laughed.

"I'm starving!" I said.

We ended up getting McDonald's drive-through and eating in the car. When we finally made it to the ski resort, we put on our ski boots, got our tickets, and then hauled our skis over to the lodge. I was thankful that I had my own skis. My mom had bought them for me for my fifteenth birthday. We used to go skiing all the time when I was little, almost every weekend in the winter when we lived in Grass Valley, but that was before it happened. I started to feel my nose prickle and an ache in my chest. I had to give myself a pep talk.

No, stop it, Lindsay. Don't go there. Don't think about it. You are here to have fun. This is fun. You love skiing. That isn't even your life anymore. Forget it.

"Hey, you ready?" Collin said. He had his skis on and was fiddling with the cuffs of his jacket, trying to get them tucked into his gloves.

"Yeah," I said. I had gone into autopilot and couldn't even remember putting all my gear on. "I guess so."

"Okay, let's go shred that mountain now! Woo hoo!" he said and did his usual howl, which always cracked me up.

We skied practically every run, and I was pleasantly surprised that we had the same skill level. He told me that before his parents had divorced, they used to go to Tahoe and Vail every winter. I'd never been to Vail, I only knew that was where rich people skied. I knew we weren't rich because my mom had had to work in the ticket booth in the morning in order to be able to get free tickets to ski in the afternoon.

By mid-afternoon, we were starving again and decided to call it quits. We got some lunch and then headed home.

forty-one

1990

After that trip, the school year sped up. It was a blur of exams, essays, and college applications. Collin and I were getting closer than ever, and since he was picking me up for school almost every day, I was tardy a lot less, so my mom didn't have to get on my case as much. In fact, she even stopped bugging me about spending so much time with Collin, but she did still make me go to the shrink, though now it was only once a month. I think she realized that Collin and I really were meant to be together. We even applied to some of the same colleges so that we could still be together after graduation. We were planning a trip to visit Northridge because we both got accepted there, and my mom was okay with it. I had drifted apart from Lainey, Anna, and Jess, though. We never hung out at school anymore, and I never saw them on the weekends. The only time I got to talk to Lainey was during art class.

It was already May, and the prom was only a couple of weeks away. I had been wondering about what Collin and I were going to do before and after and if we would even be included in Lainey's pre- and post-party plans when she asked me about it.

"So, Lindsay, how's it hangin'? You and Collin still hot and heavy?"

"Ha ha! Yes, I guess that's what you could call it."

"You guys are going to the prom, right?"

"I think so. We haven't bought the tickets yet, but, yeah, I want to go. I mean, it *is* our senior prom. Aren't you going? Do you have a date?"

"Hell yeah, I'm going. But no, Darren Yanaguchi still doesn't know I exist, so I do not have a date, per se. A bunch of us girls are just going to go as a group."

"Oh. That's cool. Did you want to plan something for before and after together?"

"Well, that's just it. We figured Collin would feel awkward being the only guy, so we decided that it would be a GONO."

"A GONO?"

"Yeah, you know, a girls only night out. A GONO."

"Oh, yeah. I guess that makes sense," I said, and there it was—Lainey had finally given up on me. I was trying to hide my disappointment, but she knew me too well and could sense it in my voice.

"But don't worry, we can still hang out on the dance floor," she said, and I could tell she was trying to cheer me up.

"Yeah, that'll be fun," I said, more to convince myself than anything. "I have to go to the bathroom." I spent the rest of the class period in the bathroom wiping away my tears to look presentable and not like I had just spent the last twenty minutes balling my eyes out, especially since Collin and I now had English together. When I finally got to class, Collin handed me a note.

Lindsay,

Well here I am, sitting in English on time before you arrived late Lindsay (Just Kiddin') If you come at all, I don't know. Well, lets suggest I pick a different thing to talk about besides your excessive lateness ok?!!!

I can't wait for the prom – Wooo – Weee

Where do you want to go to dinner – When you write me back you can let me know ok?

We have to book reservations for a hotel after school ok? By the way, I forget what's going on after school. Did you want to do something?

Lindsay, I love you so much. You know that, you better because I don't believe you so I'm gonna have to kiss you all over. Lindsay – look at me – and I'll blow you a kiss "whenever you are reading this note." I'm so stoked that I'm soon gonna be driving some VW with you in it sweetie. Well once again, I can't wait 'till Northridge and I can't stop thinking about you.

I Love You Cutie,

Collin

I finished reading the note and peeked over to look at him. He blew me a kiss as promised. Luckily, Mr. A didn't see us, as he probably would have given us detention or something. He already had to split us up and put us on opposite sides of the classroom. That note had come at just the right time, though. I was still so depressed about Lainey's GONO, but now I was thinking it could be fun, just the two of us going to prom. It would be like a fancy romantic date. After class, Collin came over to my desk to wait for me to pack up my stuff. When I stood up, he gave me a hug, which helped to cheer me up even more.

"Take it outside, you two," Mr. A said.

We laughed and ran out of the room.

"So, what are we doing today after school?" Collin said.

"Let's go get our tickets and then go to your house and plan the prom," I said.

"Sweet!"

forty-two

We decided we would make reservations at the Carnelian Room in San Francisco because the prom was going to be at the Fairmont Hotel, which was about a ten-minute walk, and we'd reserve a room at the Fairmont. I was so excited because I had been to the Carnelian Room once before with my mom and my grandparents to celebrate their anniversary. It was the fanciest restaurant I had ever been to, the kind with white tablecloths and napkins and all of the forks and spoons and knives on the table. I had to concentrate on what fork to use whenever they brought out food. Every time I took a sip of water, there was a guy standing behind me that would fill up my glass again.

My mom was actually excited about it, too, which was surprising because I knew she didn't like Collin. She took me dress shopping at Neiman Marcus in San Francisco since this occasion called for a nice dress, not the usual cheap ones I got at the mall. I tried on every single dress in my size and finally decided on a strapless, black-and-white, drop-waisted little number. It had a black top fitted to about the hip, and then it had a tiered ruffle mini skirt in black and white swirly fabric. My mom said it looked like they'd made it just for me, so she bought it for me. I couldn't believe it, it was four hundred dollars.

The day of the prom, my mom took me to get my hair done at her salon. I decided to go with a sleek blow-out, which turned out amazing. My make-up was perfect, my dress and shoes were perfect. I wish I could say the evening was perfect.

My mom and I were excited, and when I came down the stairs all glammed up, she almost started crying. We took about a thousand pictures while waiting for Collin to pick me up. When he finally got to our house, my mom wanted to take a bunch more pictures of the two of us all decked out. I could sense that Collin didn't really want to stick around that long. He seemed agitated and uncomfortable, so I told my mom that we didn't want to be late for our dinner reservation, and we left. I think my mom was only able to take like three pictures, and I could tell she was disappointed. When we got in the car, I confronted Collin about it, which was a bad idea.

"You seemed kind of annoyed back there," I said.

"Uh, yeah. Your mom hates me. I didn't like the way she was looking at me," he said.

"I don't think she hates you, she just thinks I should spend some more time with my girlfriends."

"Exactly, she's always trying to split us apart, just like my dad."

"She was really excited about me going to the prom with you. She bought me this dress and everything," I said. I couldn't figure out why he seemed to want to pick a fight about this.

"She doesn't really care about us, she's just trying to make herself look good. She doesn't understand us and wants us to break up," he said and cranked up the radio.

I didn't really know what to say to that, and it seemed like he was done talking about it. We just sat there, not talking almost the whole way. I felt tears coming on, and I didn't want to ruin this night. I had been planning it and looking forward to it for so long. We both had.

"I'm sorry, you're right," I finally said to break the silence as we approached the off-ramp into downtown San Francisco. We came to a stoplight.

"I just love you so much, I can't stand anyone who will stand in our way," he said and looked me in the eye.

"I know," I said, and he leaned in to kiss me. We got so wrapped up in the moment, we didn't even hear the cars behind us honking.

"Woo hoo!" Collin said and stepped on the gas.

After driving around the block three times and almost going the wrong way down a one-way street, we finally made it to the hotel. We parked and then walked up the block to the restaurant. It was on the top floor of a super tall building. When the doors to the elevator opened up to the restaurant, I felt a bit out of place even though I was dressed up. Most of the people there were my mom's age or older. There was a big table in the back with what looked like other prom-goers, but we didn't know them.

They sat us at a small table near the window and were really nice. They refilled the waters just like I remembered. Collin was totally uncomfortable. He hated the fact that they stood around, hovering above us. He rushed through his dinner, finished way before me, and asked for the check right away. If he could have reached across the table to take the fork out of my hand then dragged me out of the restaurant, he would have. I wanted to stay and enjoy the moment, but I didn't say anything because he had finally calmed down from the conversation about my mom, and I didn't want to start a whole new scene.

On our walk back to the hotel, Collin suggested that we get our stuff out of the car and check in to the room because it would be too late after the prom. This I agreed with, but that was where things really went downhill.

"Wow, this room is so pretty," I said.

"Not as pretty as you," Collin said and pulled me in for a hug.

"Thanks," I said. He'd finally said something about how I looked. It sure had taken him long enough.

We went in for a full-on make-out session, and then he tried to unzip my dress.

"Whoa, whoa, whoa. Not now, after. I spent two whole hours getting ready. I don't want to mess up my hair and make-up," I said and removed his hands from the back of my dress.

"Who cares? I just want to be with you," he said and kept going for my zipper.

"NO!" I said, but it came out louder than I meant it to.

"God, why do you have to be such a bitch?" he said and pushed me away.

"I'm sorry, I didn't mean to yell. I just would rather go to the prom now and then spend time with you later. That way we won't have to rush," I said and braced for the worst.

"Fine. Let's go," he said, and I was so relieved that he didn't turn this into a big fight like he had in Tahoe.

"Awesome! Thank you," I said and gave him a kiss on the cheek. "I just need to redo my lipstick, and we can go."

forty-three

We got to the entrance of the grand ballroom where the prom was already in full swing. Collin was giving me the silent treatment, but at least he wasn't yelling or causing a scene, or worse, not even going with me. I went up to the table and turned in our tickets, and a parent volunteer handed me two wristbands. I went back to where Collin was standing and put the wristband on him, grabbed his hand, and led him into the ballroom. I just stood there in awe for a minute, taking it all in. There were about a thousand strands of tiny lights covering the entire ceiling like a twinkling light tent. There were a bunch of tall cocktail tables around the room covered in black, floor-length tablecloths, and each table had a huge bouquet of white flowers—roses and lilies. I breathed in the floral smell, enjoying it, savoring it. I knew that in about an hour, the smell would be replaced by teenage B.O.

"Lindsay! Lindsay!" I heard someone yelling my name, and before I could even turn around, someone had grabbed me from behind and dipped me.

"Lainey, oh my God!" I said.

"Lindsay! You look amazing! Your dress is awesome!" Lainey said, standing me back up and holding my arms out to get a better look at my dress.

"Thank you! You look amazing!" I said, and she really did. Her waist-length, jet-black hair was in perfect coils, and she was wearing the brightest red lipstick I had ever seen, which made her teeth seem unbelievably white. "Wow!"

"Thank you!" she said and pulled me in for a bear hug. "Hey, Collin."

"Hey," he said and stared at the floor.

"Let's go dance! You don't mind if I steal your girl," she said, and without waiting for an answer, she dragged me out to the dance floor.

I mouthed the word *Sorry* to Collin and turned to run to the dance floor with Lainey. I had a feeling he was going to be pissed, but this was my senior prom, and I wanted to have fun. Lainey wove her way through the crowded dance floor to find Anna and Jess already dancing.

"Look who I found!" Lainey said.

I gave Anna and Jess hugs, and we tried to exchange compliments, but we had to yell next to each other's ears because the music was so loud. I pretended I heard what they said and smiled and laughed.

We had danced for about three songs before I noticed Collin leaned up against the wall with his arms crossed. It was so weird, he hadn't been like this at the Grid. It was like he was determined to have a crappy time. Maybe the difference in his attitude at the Grid was because he had been stoned. I didn't know, but he really needed to snap out of it.

I waved him over to come dance with me. He shook his head, so I waved him over again. Finally, a slow song came on—"I Remember You" by Skid Row— and he walked over. Thank God they were playing a song he liked. He wasn't a huge fan of top-forty music.

I took his hand and pulled him toward me.

"Finally, a non-shitty song," he said.

I laughed and rested my cheek on his shoulder. We slow danced, and I could tell he was relaxing a bit. Lainey, Anna and Jess had bowed out to get some water. The next song came on—it was Guns and Roses, "Welcome to the Jungle." I knew he liked this song, so he stayed on the dance floor with me.

The girls made it back to the dance floor, and we began dancing in one big group, my dream come true. We were jumping around, wild and free. The DJ mixed in another song, and Lainey and I recognized it right away—it was our song, "Push It"! We freaked out and busted into our routine. I was so wrapped up in it that I didn't even notice Collin had left the dance floor.

Lainey and I were singing at the top of our lungs: "*Ooh baby baby, ba-baby baby, Yo Yo Yo Yo baby pop, yeah you come here give me a kiss, better make it fast or else I'm gonna get pissed, can't you hear the music's pumpin' hard like I wish you would now push it!*" doing our dance, and the next thing we knew, everyone had formed a circle around us and was cheering us on. It was like sixth-grade science camp except better because I knew no one would forget who I was on Monday. We started pulling people into the center and getting them to do our routine. It was seriously like a scene out of a movie. When the song was over, everyone was high fiving each other.

I looked around for Collin, but I didn't see him until I looked toward the door and saw him walking out. Crap, he was pissed again. I pulled Lainey over to tell her in her ear that I had to go. She made a frowny face and pretended that she was crying, then gave me one last dip. I ran out the door to chase after Collin.

"Collin, wait!" I said, and I saw him get in the elevator and let the doors close. Arg! I ran to the elevator and pressed the up button about a hundred times, frantic for the door to open. An elderly couple stared at me as they walked by. I looked at them, smiled and waved, then went back to pressing the button as soon as they passed.

Finally it opened, and I got in. Luckily, I remembered our floor and room number, but I realized I didn't have a key. My shoes were killing me, so I took them off, and before I could hold them together in one hand, the doors opened, and a different elderly couple was standing there staring at me. I was sure I looked like a mental patient, standing there, panting to catch my breath, barefoot with one high-heeled shoe in each hand.

"Excuse me," I said and pushed past them to run down the long, carpeted hall; the swirling print on the carpet made me dizzy.

I got to our room and knocked on the door, yelling, "Collin, Collin!"

No answer. I looked through the peephole but couldn't see anything, so I put my ear to the door and heard music blasting. I tried knocking again. I knew he was in there, but he probably couldn't hear me. I could have gone back down to the lobby and called from the front desk, but what good would that have done? If he wouldn't answer the door, he wasn't going to answer the phone, either. I probably could have gotten a ride home with Lainey, but I didn't want her to know that Collin and I were fighting. I was ashamed for her to find out that everything wasn't perfect. She would probably say, "I told you so," or something like that. Or worse, she would tell my mom, and I really didn't want that to happen.

I was so exhausted all of a sudden. I sat down and leaned my back up against the door. I couldn't hold back my tears anymore. I put my face in my hands and cried. *Why is this happening to me? Why is Collin acting this way? He says he loves me, but he gets so angry. Is it my fault? Was I ignoring him? Did I push him away?* My head felt heavy.

Nightmares and reality fought in my mind. I was afraid of the dark, but right now it wasn't dark. It was not night, it was day. There were no guardians around, no one to protect us. Instead, there were shadows looming above, the ground was moving with snakes. He came to me, touching my sacred space. I didn't want him, but I did want him. Confusion and betrayal covered me like a blanket. The snakes were crawling, sliding, gliding up. I couldn't stop their hunger. I cried like a distant dove. I went outside of myself. I saw the snakes swirling up the canopy, dropping on my body like bombs. Each touch was a dagger, cutting me. I screamed out, *No!* but I had no voice, and he couldn't hear me. He was smiling, whispering secrets I was too young to know about, I did not want to know about. Having only been on this earth twelve times around the sun, how did he know the secrets of the guardians?

He departed. The room was empty now, the air sucked out, the snakes gone back to their hiding places, taking with them my innocence and trust. I imagined in the night he was cut off and bleeding somewhere. I awakened knowing the danger. I warned the guardians, but I was shushed. I knew something would happen, and it did. He was gone from this world forever, and it was not a dream. I was back inside myself again with my eyes blurred, my skull crushing, my stomach churning. There was a storm that would not calm; it was pounding me. It was my fault—I had not told enough. He had been punished. The guardians were grieving, seeking solace. They did not know what I knew, did not believe in my depths for I was too young to feel. They did not know that I felt everything. I felt my own pain and theirs, too. I was the ocean, vast and clear on the surface, teeming and bursting underneath.

I couldn't breathe. I was choking. Someone was shaking me and calling my name. I opened my eyes. I was lying on the floor on the swirly carpet of the hotel, sweating. I looked up; it was Collin who was saying my name. I didn't understand what was happening at first.

"Lindsay, you were asleep," he said.

I didn't say anything. I had nothing to say. I never had anything to say. I deserved this. It was my fault. I should have said something. I never said what I was feeling. I just let things happen.

"I'm sorry," he said. "I just was hurt because you were dancing with everyone else." His eyes looked red.

"I'm sorry. I didn't mean to ignore you. It's just that it was the prom, you know," I said and sat up.

"Come on, it's two a.m., we still have the rest of the night. Let's smoke a bowl," he said, and I got up and followed him back in the room. I didn't really want to smoke pot, but I went along with it because I was too tired to argue.

forty-four

Collin called the next afternoon and wanted me to come over and hang out. I decided to go because I felt like we needed some time alone together without all the prom craziness. What we needed was just to hang out together like we used to, joking around, listening to music, and laughing. He was staying at his mom's again, and she was at work, so we had the place to ourselves for a little bit.

Collin plopped down on the step near the sliding glass door leading to the patio. I sat down next to him.

"Look what I still have left over from the prom." He pulled out a baggie with a joint in it and dangled it in front of my face.

"What time did you say your mom would be home?" I said.

"Two hours," he said.

"Oh, okay, cool," I said, not really wanting to get high, but we could always move to his garage room after, and his mom wouldn't bother us, especially after the last time. Plus, Collin seemed really happy, and I knew we would definitely be laughing soon, so I agreed to smoke it with him. He lit it up and took a huge toke, then passed it to me. We sat there staring at the trees just beyond the patio for a while, passing the joint back and forth. When it was almost done, Collin crushed it out on the cement step, leaned back, and put it in his front jeans pocket.

"Save that for later," he said, and for some reason I thought that was the funniest thing I had ever heard.

I cracked up, which caused him to crack up. The next thing I knew, we were making out. It was nice until he wanted to just go at it right there halfway on the living room carpet and halfway on the cement step.

"No, not here," I said and pushed him off of me. As if a switch had flipped in his brain, he immediately stopped smiling. I could tell he was about to snap. So I said, "Let's go in the garage." I got up before he could catch me.

"Fine," he said, but I could tell he was still pissed.

I walked to the door of the garage and opened it. Inside was pitch black, so I fumbled for the light switch. The next thing I remember is feeling a blow to my back. My wrists hit the doorjambs, and I landed on my side on the hard cement floor. Then Collin was holding me and crying and saying, "I'm sorry" over and over again.

I knew what to do, always. My gut, my intuition, my heart, whatever you want to call it, told me, but I didn't listen. Why didn't I listen? Why didn't I trust myself? I didn't trust myself. I didn't trust myself to just observe and know. I made a lot of mistakes. I made bad choices, choices that I knew would hurt me.

I decided to keep dating Collin even though he'd pushed me down the steps. It had only been three steps that led out into the garage, but still, he'd pushed me. That should have been a red flag. I should have listened to my gut and run out the door. But instead, I stayed and accepted his apology. I looked into his watery green eyes and accepted that jerk's apology. He was giving me a load of crap, saying he would never do it again and how sorry he was, blah, blah, blah, blah…. Seriously, I knew how it worked. I'd watched my parents do this whole cycle-of-abuse dance before. I should have known better. I did know better. I was a freakin' honor student, so why was I allowing this to happen?

Emotions swirled around and within me like leaves on the Santa Ana winds on a hot fall day, and it didn't make sense. It shouldn't have been hot and windy, but it was. Nature took over, and I allowed it to envelop me in its force. I was powerless to the gravitational pull, as it was stronger than I was. It seemed stronger than I would ever be. Would I ever be strong? Would I have the strength to listen to my gut? Would I be able to pull away from the Santa Anas? Would I be able to stand up? Stand up for what I knew was right? Stand up to people who were trying to hold me down? Stand up for myself?

As he was talking to me, I knew what I needed to do. I knew what was right. I knew, but I couldn't do it.

"So, how was the prom?" Dr. Ross asked and pushed his glasses up higher on his nose with his index finger.

"It was great, really fun," I said, which was true. The actual prom had been fun, it was just the before that had been awkward and the after that had been a total disaster. I definitely did not want to get into the whole ugly scene with Dr. Ross.

"I'm glad to hear that. Where did you end up going to dinner?" he said.

"We went to the Carnelian Room," I said. Ugh, seriously, were we going to play twenty questions?

"Ooh, fancy," he said.

"Yeah, it was really nice," I said. Okay, I guessed we were talking about this now.

"I'm more of a burger joint kind of guy, the way they fill the water glass after one sip always makes me feel uncomfortable," he said and chuckled.

"I think my boyfriend would agree with you. He's not into restaurants with tablecloths. Come to think of it, he's not really into restaurants with tables. He would rather just drive-through and eat in his car," I said and laughed.

Dr. Ross laughed, too, and then sighed.

We sat there for a moment not talking until finally I blurted out, "I had another dream."

"Oh?" he said.

"Well, not a dream, but more of a nightmare."

"Hmmm."

"I used to have it when I was little."

"I see, you've had this nightmare before?"

"Yes, there were snakes again, but there was also someone."

"Hmmm, do you remember who it was?"

"I don't know, maybe."

"Was this person someone you know?"

"Kind of, I guess," I said and felt my heart beating faster and sweat forming on my upper lip. It was so stuffy in his office. A plume of smoke from the incense burning on top of the file cabinet hung in the air. I pushed up the sleeve of my sweatshirt and then immediately pulled it back down to cover my arm, remembering why I was wearing a sweatshirt in June. I didn't want to talk about him. I pushed him out of my mind. I felt my eyes water.

"Okay, so this is a real person in your nightmare? Can you talk about what happened in the dream?" he said.

I took a deep breath to keep the tears from spilling out. "Yes. I'm in my room, and it seems like daytime, but it's dark. I see a shadow come toward me, and then the shadow is on my bed. I want to scream, but I can't. I want to run away, but the floor is covered with snakes, and then he's gone. And then I see him somewhere else, and something bad happens to him. He is bleeding, and there is just blood everywhere." I took another deep breath, but this time a fat teardrop escaped. I didn't want to cry. I didn't want to feel this again.

Dr. Ross nudged the tissue box toward me. I took a tissue and held it with both hands, pressing it into my eyes. The room felt hot, like the air had been sucked out of it. I had to tell myself to breathe in and out.

"Did this person hurt you?" Dr. Ross said.

I couldn't talk. I took another deep breath.

"Lindsay, you're safe here. No one can hurt you now. It's okay."

"He touched me." Another deep breath. "He touched my private parts." Breathe, breathe, breathe.

"Is this person still hurting you?"

"No."

"Is this person a man who lived with you?"

"No. I mean, yes, but he wasn't a man. He was my mom's boyfriend's son."

"Did you tell anyone about this?"

"No," I said and couldn't hold back the tears. Snot oozed out of my nose. I took more tissues and covered my face and sobbed loudly into the wad of tissues.

Dr. Ross waited for me to calm down before he said anything. "How did you get him to stop?" he asked.

How did I get him to stop? That was such a loaded question, I didn't want to answer it. All of my memories that I had been denying came flooding back to me: my mom breaking up with her boyfriend, Bruce, and leaving me with my grandparents to find a new job, a new place, a new life. The real-life nightmare that brought her back, Adam. Adam, who I never saw again. Adam, who went to a sleepover. Adam, who got sick. Adam, who went to the hospital. Adam, whose body stopped working. Adam, whose heart stopped. Adam, who had a pacemaker put in. Adam, who the doctors couldn't save. Adam, who was thirteen years old. Adam, who died. Adam, whom I wanted to like me. Adam, who used to touch my private parts when our parents weren't around. Adam, whom I wished would be punished. Adam that I couldn't bring back. Adam that my mom couldn't bring back. Adam that Bruce couldn't bring back. Adam that couldn't save their relationship.

It was my fault. I wished he would be punished, but I didn't tell anyone. I only told God. God punished him, and it was my fault. My mom moved away again and left me with Bruce. Bruce, who turned white, his hair, his face. Bruce, who couldn't talk anymore. I thought if I could just be good then he could start talking again, but he couldn't.

I had headaches. I had headaches. I had headaches. I lay alone in my bed with the curtains closed in the dark every day. My mom brought me to live with her near her new job, in the new place, in the new life. My head ached. She made me visit my dad. My head ached. She sent me to live with my grandparents. They gave me ice cream sundaes. They put a piece of plywood on their living room floor so that I could tap dance in the house. I tap danced. They helped me forget about what had happened. I buried it deep. That was how I got it to stop.

"He died," I said, feeling numbness and stinging pain all at the same time. I had buried these memories so deep for so long that it felt like they were from someone else's life. I was sitting on the sofa, but it was someone else who was talking.

"Oh, I see," Dr. Ross said. "Did this happen recently?"

"No. It happened eight years ago." I said it so matter-of-factly, like I was a news reporter just reporting the news. I stopped crying; I had no more tears left. I stopped feeling. I had trained myself not to think about this or feel anything about it and just switch into zombie mode.

Dr. Ross just sat there, quiet for a long time, before he said, "You know, Lindsay, people who go through things like this sometimes blame themselves. Do you think you have been blaming yourself for what happened?"

I couldn't answer. I couldn't talk anymore. I was still a zombie watching some other girl sitting on the sofa.

He continued, "Sometimes when we blame ourselves, we think we don't deserve to be happy. We think we deserve to be mistreated. We seek out other people who are hurting and stay in relationships with them even though we know they aren't right so we can continue to punish ourselves."

I was hearing what he was saying, but I wasn't fully listening to him. My brain had shut down, and all I could do was stare at the books on the shelves.

We sat there just breathing for a long time before the timer finally dinged.

forty-five

I managed to make it home. I managed to make it up the stairs. I managed to make it into the bathroom where I stripped off my clothes to get the smell of incense and any reminder of being in that office off of me. I wanted to wash it all away: the memories, the conversation. But his words were stuck in my head like a broken record: *"We seek out other people who are hurting to punish ourselves."* Was that what I was doing? The water from the shower was blasting me in the face, but the words wouldn't wash away. Was I punishing myself? I deserved it, though. Didn't I? I had been trying to forget for so long. Was it possible that my ten-year-old self had taken the blame for Adam's death? I did take the blame, I felt guilty and ashamed. I felt guilty for asking God to punish him, and I felt ashamed because I'd let him touch me. I think deep down I let him touch me because I wanted him to like me. I liked the attention he gave me. I thought it was all my fault, and I deserved to be punished. I spent the last eight years seeking out people who would punish me. I always found people that wanted to do bad things. I found them and let them punish me.

I was startled by a knock on the door and my stepdad's voice.

"Hey, Lindsay, lay off the hot water, or I'm going to shut it off!" I heard his laughter growing faint as he walked away.

Holy crap! I needed to pull myself together.

A week later, I was having dinner at the dining room table with my mom and stepdad.

"Hey, good news, we're going to be chaperones for the Grad Night Party! Isn't that great, kid!" Chip said and slapped me on the back.

My brain froze—what had he just said?

"She doesn't look happy," my mom said.

"Wha oo you ean?" he said with his mouth full. He finished chewing and said, "Everybody loves us! Linds, you don't want us to go?"

They were both staring at me now, waiting for an answer. What was I supposed to say? There was no way in hell I wanted my parents following me around at Grad Night. Wasn't it obvious? I mean, really, at that point I didn't even want to go. Collin didn't even like coming over to our house to see my parents on a regular day. I couldn't even imagine how pissed he'd be when he found out. Seriously, I didn't even blame him. Grad Night, *Grad* Night, the night after our graduation…where we are supposed to be *adults.* Chaperones—*really?* Ugh, I couldn't believe this. This was horrible.

"Lindsay, what's wrong?" my mom said.

What wasn't wrong? Was she kidding me right now? I literally could not speak, and I had completely lost my appetite.

"I have to go," I said. Her words had made me want to vomit. I got up, took my plate to the sink, ran to the upstairs bathroom, and locked the door behind me. I sat on the floor in front of the toilet and flipped back the seat with a loud clang against the tank. I pushed up the sleeves of my sweatshirt, looked at the bruises on my forearms, and then stared into the empty toilet. I took a deep breath, causing the water to blur my faint reflection. The nausea has subsided, but I still sat there contemplating my life.

I decided to pretend that I was okay with my mom and stepdad being Grad Night chaperones. I just didn't have the energy to fight about it anymore, and besides, it was a done deal. There was nothing I could do about it. My mom bought me this cute white dress to wear to graduation. It was fitted, just above knee length, and had little cap sleeves.

She also called Collin's mom and invited her and Collin to our house for a pre-graduation lunch, which saved me from having to have the conversation about them being chaperones with Collin. I was shocked when they accepted, but more shocked that my mom was making an effort to get to know Collin and his family. Where had all this "family get together" crap been when I'd first started going out with him?

My mom also invited my grandparents, my aunt and cousin, and my real dad. Talk about awkward. There we were, all standing around drinking iced tea, balancing our plates of Chinese chicken salad, and talking about how lucky we were to be having nice weather. My whole family ignored the giant elephant in the room—the fact that my biological father was a recovering asshole and a practicing alcoholic—and continued to make small talk about nothing.

After almost everyone was finished eating, my mom thought it would be a good idea to open my graduation gifts. I didn't think this was a good idea with Collin and his mom there, but I wasn't in the mood to put up a fight. It was awkward, but Collin and his mom seemed okay with it. They were actually pleasant, smiling and commenting on how nice the gifts were. I mean, Collin's mom had always been nice, but it was as if someone had opened up the roof, snatched Collin out, and replaced him with a look alike, because he usually wasn't that friendly when adults were around. It gave me hope, I guess, that someday we could be happy, and our two families could get together for special occasions.

That was the last pleasant moment of the day. First there was the cringe-worthy kiss goodbye from my dad—his mustache grossed me out. Then came the unbearable line we had to wait in to get into the auditorium for graduation. They'd made us arrive an hour early just to stand in the blazing hot sun, and afterward came the even more unbearable graduation ceremony, where the principal droned on about how wonderful the class of 1990 was. He could have fooled me, where had all of this praise been when we'd actually been in school?

When they started calling names, I got excited because I knew it was almost over and we could get to the celebrating part. Even with my mom and Chip there, I was determined to have a good time and avoid them like the plague.

After what seemed like an eternity and all 418 students' names had been called, everyone poured out of the auditorium and into the parking lot. I didn't see Collin right away, but I found Lainey, Anna, and Jess. Lainey gave me a giant bear hug, and a flood of emotion came over me. The realization that I wouldn't be seeing her in art class every day anymore hit me hard, and I felt actual pain in my chest. My eyes felt warm as they filled with tears. When she pulled away from me, there was no hiding my emotions.

"Lindsay, don't cry! This is the fun part!" Lainey said.

"I know, it's just...I just love you guys," I said.

Lainey came in for another bear hug. "We love you, too, and now it's time to par-tay!" She started in on our "Push It" routine.

"Wait, I forgot to tell you that my parents will be chaperones," I said, grabbing her arm to get her to stop dancing.

"Uh-oh." Lainey froze mid hip thrust. "Um, I see your problem, but don't worry, we'll keep them occupied, wink, wink," she said just as Collin came jogging over.

"Hey. I got some party favors from Dan," Collin said.

"You know they search everyone before we get on the bus, right?" Jess said.

"Not a problem," Collin said and patted his crotch.

"Uhh, gross," Anna said and pretended to gag.

"Hey, look, everyone's lining up for the buses, we gotta go!" Lainey said and hooked elbows with Anna and Jess. "See you on the boat!"

"Bye!" I said.

Collin put his arm around me, and we walked toward the bus. Jess was right, they gave all the guys a pat down and made us girls open our purses so they could check them for alcohol and drugs. Luckily, it was probably a felony to grab the crotch of a student, so we made it on the bus without incident. By the time we got on the bus, it was already in full party mode. Someone had had the bright idea of balling up the graduation programs, and everyone was throwing them at each other and singing a song we normally sang at the end of football games when we were winning. It definitely seemed appropriate now—we were winning, and we were done with high school.

"Na na na na, na na na na, hey hey hey, goodbye!"

That went on for what seemed like an eternity until we finally made it to San Francisco and the pier where our ferry was waiting to take us on a five-hour cruise of the bay. Yes, five hours. Five hours of avoiding my mom and Chip. I was trying to make sure I avoided their check in line, but no such luck.

"Hi, name please?" Chip said.

"Ha, ha, very funny," I said.

"What, I'm just trying to be inconspicuous," he said in a loud whisper with the back of his hand covering the side of his mouth.

"Thanks," I said and let him stamp my hand.

Collin stepped up behind me.

"Hi, Collin," Chip said.

"Hi," Collin said, offering his hand for the stamp and staring off to the side.

"You guys are all set. Have fun!"

"Thanks." We walked as fast as we could to get as far away from them as possible. We hadn't even been there for five minutes before Collin said, "I'm going to use the restroom, and then you can use the restroom."

"Ah, okay, got it," I said, knowing he was talking about smoking the "party favors" he'd brought but not really sure how it was going to go down, since it would probably stink up the whole boat. I was feeling extremely uneasy about his plan, but at that point I would have rather gotten kicked off the boat then have had Collin mad at me. I could always just pretend to smoke it. I wondered if he would even notice if the joint wasn't smaller. I mean, if he was stoned, there was a good chance I could pull it off.

Collin gave me a kiss and disappeared into the bathroom. There was a mirror in the narrow hallway, so I pulled out my lip gloss to pass the time. People kept walking by, and I tried to avoid making eye contact with anyone so I didn't have to answer any questions. I got a whiff of that skunky pot smell. Oh crap, you could smell it. There was no way I wanted to add to that.

"Woo hoo! Now it's a party!" Collin said, coming out of the bathroom and pulling me in for a hug to pass the "party favor" to me. I took it, shoved it in my purse, and walked into the bathroom. It was full of girls at the mirrors, and there were only two stalls, and they were both full. This was good, I'd have to wait until a stall cleared, so it would seem like I had been in there long enough to smoke, and Collin wouldn't get suspicious. I figured I might as well actually pee while I was in there. After waiting for the girls to clear the sink area, I'd been in there for a good ten minutes total. I popped a mint to make it seem like I was covering up my smoky pot breath. When I came out, I knew I had to put on a good show.

"Duuude, that was strong!" I said and pulled him in for a hug to hand him back the baggie. There was no way I wanted to get caught with it in my purse, I did not need that nightmare scenario.

"Do you want a mint? These are the best mints in the world. MMMMMM!" I said to drive home the stoned act—everything was the "best thing in the world" when you were stoned.

"Yeah, thanks, I got cotton mouth like a motherf'er!" he said, and I handed him a mint.

"Yeah, me, too!" I said.

He popped the mint in his mouth. "Holy shit! This *is* the best mint in the world!" He started laughing. I had to laugh, too, or he would know something was up, but it actually was kind of funny. Then I heard a loud horn and felt the boat moving.

"Woo hoo!" Collin howled again.

"Woo hoo!" I said. I could hear that the DJ had already started up because the bass was making the boat vibrate with a steady, *Boom, boom, boom, boom, boom*.

"Let's go dance!" I said and grabbed his wrist to pull him along. I didn't want to give him a chance to object because I wasn't taking no for an answer. The room was already packed with heads bobbing to the beat. The ceiling was pretty low, so some of the taller guys could actually touch it and were jumping up and slapping it. The sun hadn't gone down yet, so you could only see a faint glow of the electric blue and hot pink spotlights in the corners. The dance floor was so packed that it overflowed onto the brown carpet surrounding the room, and we had to squeeze through the crowd to get to the actual dance floor. Large windows lined either side of the room and had thick, wooden, dark brown frames you could almost sit on, and people had already started using them as shelves—they were lined with abandoned plastic cups. Out of the window, I saw the hazy skyline of San Francisco and the wharf getting smaller as the ferry chugged its way into the bay.

The DJ was mixing classic house music, which was not Collin's favorite at all, but they started playing "Pump up the Volume" by MARRS, and there was no way I wasn't going to dance. Plus, it seemed like everyone had moved into the room, so there was no place for Collin to go. We were like sardines. I didn't care anymore if he was mad, I just let the music take over. I put my hands up over my head and started jumping up and down to the beat. Lainey found me and jumped her way over to me with Anna and Jess. There weren't a lot of lyrics, but we were singing them.

"Pump up the volume, pump up the volume, pump up the volume, dance, dance! Put the needle on the record, and the drum beats go like this!"

I lost track of Collin again, but this time I knew he couldn't have left since we were all stuck on the boat. The DJ kept his "get pumped" theme going with "Pump up the Jam" by Technotronic, and everyone went nuts with more screaming and jumping.

"I want a place to stay, get your booty on the floor tonight, make my day! Yo, pump up the jam, pump it up while your feet are stompin' and the jam is pumping, look ahead the crowd is jumpin'!" We kept singing, "Make my day, make my day! Maaaaake my day, make my, make my, make my daaaaay!"

I didn't know if it was all the jumping or the heat from all of the bodies packed in that small room, but I started feeling like I might pass out. I figured I was probably dehydrated, so I bounced my way to the edge where the (non-alcoholic) bar was, filled a cup with water, and guzzled it down. As I was going for a refill, I felt someone tugging on my arm.

It was Collin, and he didn't look happy. He was yelling something, but I couldn't hear him over the loud music. I pantomimed walking with my fingers and pointed outside. There were some stairs that led up to a rooftop seating area that had rows of benches. I was worried we might bump into my mom and Chip, but it was a chance I had to take in order to calm down the situation. Collin and I squeezed through the crowd to the door, and before we could even get up the stairs, Collin was yelling again.

"What the hell, Lindsay? Why did you ditch me like that?" Collin said. His face was red, he had veins popping out of his neck, and the green parts of his eyes weren't green anymore—his pupils had taken over, and his eyes had turned completely black. I had seen him mad before, but this was much worse than anything I had seen. It was scary, he reminded me of my dad when he got mad, and I had a flashback to when he took a belt out, grabbed Caleb by the arm, and dragged him into the bathroom. There had been yelling and crying and then screaming, and I'd run to the bedroom and put a pillow over my head so I couldn't hear it anymore. Later, when everything had calmed down and Caleb had fallen asleep crying in his bed, I'd gone to the bathroom and seen red marks on the wall that looked like blood.

What was I doing here with Collin? It had been so bizarre earlier today seeing both Collin and my dad in the same room. They had both been pretending to be normal when clearly they were not. I felt like I had just entered the *Twilight Zone*, where you kept meeting the same person over and over and couldn't escape. There was a room filled with doors, but when you opened them, it was just outer space. I knew I needed to get out of this room and away from them, but I didn't know how to do it.

I couldn't just jump off the boat, although at that moment I really wanted to. The only thing I could think of was to apologize and make something up to get Collin to calm down so we could get through this night without a scene, but it was too late. Just as I was about to say I was sorry and I hadn't meant to ditch him, Lainey walked up with Anna and Jess behind her. They didn't say anything, they just stood there staring at us. The sight of them snapped Collin out of Hulk mode, and the veins in his neck went away.

His face was still kind of red when he said, "Hey, what's up?" and nodded to Lainey.

"Nothing, what's up with you?" she said with her brow furrowed. They stood there staring each other down, and I felt like I needed to say something or we might spend the rest of the night is this awkward stand-off.

"Hey, Lainey, we were just getting some air," I said, trying to sound happy and upbeat and not like I had just been about to have the worst fight of my life.

"Uh huh, okay, well, we'll be down on the lower level with your *parents* if you need us," she said and gave one last glare at Collin. Then the three of them walked past us and down the stairs.

"Let's go sit upstairs and get some air," I said and took Collin's hand.

He didn't say anything and let me lead him up the stairs. I guess my friends had snapped him back to reality and he'd realized he couldn't go into a rage in front of all of these people. When we got to the top deck, I saw a bench way in the back that was partially obscured by a giant vent pipe thingy. Perfect. We sat down on opposite ends of the bench.

Obviously, he was still angry, but he wasn't yelling. Now was my chance to smooth things over.

"Collin, I'm sorry. I didn't mean to ditch you. You know how I love to dance, and it was just so crowded," I said, holding my hair back in one hand to keep the wind from blowing it in my face. I scooted a little closer to him, partially because I wanted him to calm down, and partially because it was getting a little chilly, and I needed some body warmth.

"I know, it's just that I love you so much, and I can't stand being apart from you or sharing you with anyone," he said. Well, that explained why he'd never wanted to be with my friends.

"I know. I love you, too," I said, but as the words came out of my mouth, I wondered if they were true or if I was just in lust with him and drawn to the drama. I kept hearing Dr. Ross' words in my head: *We find people who are hurting to punish ourselves.*

I was actually shivering now; my flimsy little white graduation dress was not keeping me warm at all. Collin scooted next to me and put his arm around me just like he'd done during our times at the beach. I wished we could go back to the times when we'd laughed and cuddled up next to each other. Now, it seemed like everything just ended up in a big fight.

I rested my head on his shoulder, letting my hair whip around in the wind. We sat without talking like that for the rest of the cruise.

forty-six

I felt like I must have taken a sleeping pill or something because when I rolled over to look at my clock radio, it said 3:00 p.m.! I had slept for a solid twelve and half hours. After the cruise ended, we'd had to take the buses back to school, and then it took some time to get back home because my mom and Chip had to wait until everyone left before they could leave. We ended up not getting home until about 2:30 a.m.

I rolled back over and stared up at the ceiling. I moved to straighten my legs and felt something hit my foot at the end of my bed. I tilted my head up to look, and I saw a pile of clothes and my yearbook sitting on the end of my bed. Wow, I must have been so out of it last night I hadn't even bothered to clear off my bed before I'd gotten in it.

I shimmied down to grab my yearbook. I had been so busy taking finals leading up to graduation that I hadn't read what people had written to me. I flipped right to the back and saw Collin's friends' messages.

Lindsay,

Stay sweet. I don't think that should be too hard. It's only been a year I've known you but it seems longer. Don't let Collin give you a hard time. Tell him I said that. Remember don't hassle it!

Your Friend,

Josh the Great

Lindsay,

Well I'm glad we became better acquainted. This year went by too quick. Anyways, wish you and Collin the best. Stay yourself. And kick Collins ass if he gets out of hand. Have a great summer and wish you luck in the future.

Love,

Jake

Huh, they had both kind of said the same thing. Was it that obvious? I kept reading.

Lindsay,

Well beautiful, it's been a long four years but we finally made it. Even though Pom Pom wasn't the best experience of my life the one good thing that came out of it was the special friendships we all share with each other. All I have to say is that Paula Abdul better watch out because Lindsay Trifling is one HOT little Chickita that is ready to strut her stuff. I still wish you were going to Long Beach with me so we could dance together. But Northridge is close enough for us to party together. I'm gonna miss you so much next year but I know we'll keep in touch.

♡ ya tons,

Charlotte

I was going to miss her, too. We'd made a really great team. It would have been fun to have gone to college with her, but I had already committed to go to Northridge with Collin. Now, I was having second thoughts. I kept reading.

Lindsay – Binsychan – Well, I guess I can grace your page, I'm so generous! ☺ Well 3

313

yrs 2gether w/Ragin x's 2 remember! 2 BAD the last yr we didn't go out as much, but I <u>ALWAYS</u> remember driving, sizzlers, drinking, my house, Oh yes and speak of the devil, Bill Warner, ooh I'm so jealous of you I WANTED HIM, JK Yeah rt! Well, I hope we keep in touch, cuz I've really missed going out with you and just bull shittin! My problems, Darren – Yuck! I'd rather not remember OUR OBSESSION W/ HAIR! I'm sorry, RT now I'm so blocked up. So save this page - & I'll see you in the summer. You'd better call and make sure Collin takes care of U!

♡ Lainey, to be cont…

Oh my god, that was so Lainey to not even finish. I had to read it three times to understand her writing. She was right, though, we hadn't gone out as much this past year.

Then I got to Anna's, and I got really sad.

Lindsay – Bobinsy – NA NA NA – loobinsy – what the hell ever! Geeze, I don't know. Anyways it's too bad we kind of drifted apart – thanks to Collin, but I'm glad you found that special someone, finally after the Monday, Tue, Wed, Thur, Fri, Sat and Sunday man. Thanks for being another friend who is a winner and going to a real college. J/K. Well next year. I hope you stop getting all the guys and start saving some for the rest of us. We never doubled, oh well. Next year. I want you to promise me that if you do meet Mr. Fine, you have to introduce me to his brother. J/K. I have my future husband in my hands. Do You? I hope he treats you good next year. Don't hold yourself back from the other guys 'cause of him. Since Lainey never did, you still have to teach me (and Jess) how to dance. Lainey's too funky anyways. I hope in the future you become the wanna-be Paula Abdul. Call me sometime you butthead – don't let Collin steal your time! It feels like you left for college senior year.

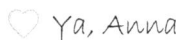 Ya, Anna

Whoa! Those last two lines stunned me. I really hadn't thought anyone had noticed or even cared that I was around less. I'd had no idea it was that obvious. Had I been so absorbed with Collin that it really seemed like I had left altogether?

I turned to the last page, and there it was, Collin's message.

Lindsay,

Hey little sweet thing!!! To start off with, I want to tell you that I love you! Just like every other note that this might sound like. Even though we have had some tough times, the good times are 99.9999% and all I ever remember. Do we fight, hell NO!!! Lindsay, you are the sweetest girl and I want you to remember that! ☺ Collin loves you, and I think I love you so much I even was in love with you from a past life. You deserve everything. Lindsay, I even have troubles thinking about my cutie ☺ because I get

And that was it. His message cut off mid-sentence. I guess class had ended before he could finish. I knew what he meant by being in love in a past life—we had this connection that I couldn't explain. But even though the good times were so good, I did remember all the fights. Was this really the life I wanted to live? Did I want to go to college with Collin? I'd thought I did. I'd thought I wanted it more than anything in the world, but now I didn't know. Charlotte was going to Long Beach, where I'd also applied and been accepted to. Collin and I had made plans this week to go visit Northridge together.

I didn't know if it was because I couldn't remember the last time I'd eaten, or what, but my stomach was in knots. Did I want to forge this path?

No, I didn't. I already knew that I couldn't continue down this path, but I still sat in this jail cell of a relationship not knowing how to break out or bust down the walls. I was searching for answers. Maybe if I went on the trip with Collin, I would be able to see if going to college with him would be the best or worst decision of my life.

But what if I went on the trip with him and didn't like it, how was I going to deal with that? It was too late to cancel the trip now, I just needed to go and get it over with. I closed my yearbook and tossed it on the floor.

forty-seven

I couldn't believe my mom was actually allowing Collin and I to visit Northridge together. She must have known this trip would teach me something—as long as it didn't kill me first—and she was right.

The plan was to drive to Southern California to visit Cal State Northridge, the only school Collin and I had both applied to, and then to stay overnight at his grandmother's house in Ontario. I had been excited about it at first; he had been behaving himself up until graduation. Maybe his interest in going away to college had gotten his parents off his back and in turn made him more relaxed, I didn't know, but the drive down was tolerable. Maybe he sensed I was having second thoughts about him, so he was doing his best to be like he'd been when we'd first met.

We actually had fun, shouting at the top of our lungs to the music on the radio like we used to when we'd first started dating. We made it to Northridge by two and spent forty minutes walking around the campus before we decided to go to his grandmother's house. I wanted to stay longer and actually go on the tour, but he was in a good mood for a change, so I decided not to rock the boat. I never knew what would set him off these days—I mean, he'd totally flipped out when I'd wanted to keep dancing at the prom and graduation. Come to think of it, he flipped out whenever I wanted to do something he didn't want to do.

Anyway, everything was going smoothly until the next day when we drove home. Collin had this idea that we should go to the beach first, which was about an hour out of the way, but what the hell, I thought, we were in Southern California and it was still early. So I agreed.

Big mistake.

I had forgotten that Collin was a big fan of PDA, and I guess he'd forgotten that I wasn't a fan. Well, maybe he wasn't thinking about PDA, he just didn't give a shit about anyone or what they thought. I, on the other hand, still had some self-respect—not a lot, but some—and it made me feel uncomfortable when he wanted to make out in front of other people. Anyway, there we were at the beach, lying on the sand in our bathing suits. To make matters worse, I had brought my florescent orange bikini, so I pretty much stuck out like a sore thumb. There was no blending in whatsoever, and he was trying to kiss me, and I noticed a family with two young children sitting a few yards away looking at us. I pushed him away.

"Not now," I said, pointing with my eyes to the family.

"I don't give a shit," he said and continued to grope me.

"I know you don't, but I do!" I said a little louder than I meant to.

The family was now full-on staring.

"Come on, Lindsay, don't pull this crap," he said.

"Let's just go somewhere else," I said, hoping he'd lose interest.

"Fine." He grabbed my arm and yanked me up.

"Ouch!" I said.

"Let's go!" he yelled.

"Shhh!" I said and then gave a weak smile to the family, gathering up my bag and towel.

"Don't tell me to shhh!" he said and pushed me to get me to walk to the car.

The dad stood up and started to walk toward me. I waved him off—he would just make Collin angrier.

Collin grabbed my wrist and dragged me up the beach. I stumbled as I tried to keep up. We finally reached his dad's black Blazer. Collin opened the door, shoved me in, and slammed the door. It was about a thousand degrees in the car, so I tried to roll down the window, but it was stuck. My bare legs were burning on the black leather seats, so I adjusted my towel under me and didn't notice Collin going around to the other side of the car to get in.

"Don't you ever do that to me again!" he yelled and grabbed me by the neck and shoved my head up against the window. I couldn't breathe, but I somehow wedged my knee up between us and used my foot to kick his chest with every ounce of strength I had.

"Get off of me!" I screamed. Stunned, he sat there and looked at me. I was now frantically trying to open the door.

"Lindsay, I'm sorry. I didn't mean it," he said and grabbed my arm.

I ripped my arm out of his grasp and fell out of the car onto the hot pavement. I got up and ran as fast as I could down the sand. He chased me. My feet were burning, and I had to stop. I collapsed back onto the sand, which was now stuck to the sweat on my body.

"Lindsay, are you okay?" he said, pretending to be concerned since every jogger and biker had stopped to look at us. I guess he had decided to give a shit about what other people thought now.

"I'm fine," I said and let him help me up. "Take me home."

We walked back to the car in silence. We both got in, and he started the car.

"I'm sorry," he said again.

"I know," I said without looking at him. I reached down, blasted the radio, and rolled down the window. He started driving. Good, we'd be home in six hours, and I'd never have to see him again.

We didn't speak the entire way home. I stared out the window watching the open grassy fields and rows of orchards go by. I couldn't even look at him. I didn't want to look at what was staring me in the face. I didn't want to admit it. I'd brought this onto myself. I'd allowed him to treat me this way. I'd allowed him to take me away from my friends. I'd allowed him to take me away from my family. I'd allowed myself to become defenseless. I'd allowed myself to believe the things he said about me. He said no one else would love me like he did. He said I must not love him if I wanted to spend time with my friends or family. He said I was stupid for thinking anyone else cared about me, and I'd believed him. I'd believed him, and I'd stopped believing in myself. I'd stopped believing in myself and allowed him to dim my light. But in the last hour, before he turned my light off completely, I'd remembered who I was, and I'd shined my light in his face, and he couldn't handle it. He was the weak one, a parasite sucking the life out of its host.

Before I got out of the car, he made one last attempt to tell me that he was sorry and to promise that it would never happen again. He told me he loved me and that was why he went crazy sometimes—because he loved me so much. He was crying. Part of me felt bad for him. I could see that he was hurting, but I had heard this before. He never kept his promises. I sat there and listened to him and realized there was nothing I could do to get him to keep his promises.

I didn't have anything left to say, so I hugged him, grabbed my bag, and got out of the car. As I walked up the front path to my house, I noticed a white Karman Ghia parked down the street. That was weird, it looked just like Anna's car, but what would she have been doing here when she knew I wasn't home?

I dug through my bag and found my keys at the bottom. I opened the door and stood there stunned for a second—I couldn't comprehend what was going on. Lainey, Anna and Jess were sitting on the sofa with my mom.

"Oh good, you're home," my mom said.

"Yeah, what's going on?" I said, feeling a little shaky. I wasn't in the mood for company. I just wanted to take a shower and crawl into bed.

"Well, honey, the girls came over because we were concerned about you," my mom said.

"Concerned about me?" I said, and the weight of everything that had happened came crashing down on me, and I crumbled to the floor and cried right there by the front door.

Lainey and Jess ran over, picked me up off the floor, walked me to the sofa, and sat on either side of me. Lainey put her arm around my shoulders and pulled me in for a side hug while Jess rubbed my back.

Anna went to the bathroom and came back with a tissue box. She said, "When we saw Collin yelling at you at Grad Night, we went down to the lower deck to talk to your mom and Chip. We told them that we thought he might be hurting you and that you could be in trouble and we didn't know what to do."

"When they came to me, it confirmed my suspicions, and I asked them to come here today so that we could talk to you about it and help you," my mom said.

"I don't know what to do," I said between sobs. "I'm afraid to break up with him." I took a tissue and buried my face in it. I felt hot, like I had a fever, and I could tell my face was bright red. Jess must have felt the heat coming from my body because she got up and got me a glass of water. I gulped it down all at once.

"We came up with a plan," my mom said. "Chip is going to call his parents and let them know that if he comes near you again, we will file charges and get a restraining order against him. Since he is eighteen, he will listen if he knows what's good for him."

"But I feel like I need to break up with him in person," I said.

"Nooooooo!" they all said together.

"You can call him and tell him, and we will sit with you while you do it in case he tries to pull a fast one and get you to come over there," Lainey said.

"So that's it. Just a phone call," I said. It felt so wrong and impersonal after all we had been through together. I was torn because I knew if I went to him, he might convince me not to break up with him, but part of me still felt bad for him and ached for the connection we'd had in the beginning of our relationship.

"Well, not exactly, there's more," my mom said.

"Yay, this is my favorite part!" Lainey said, bouncing on the sofa and doing a silent cheer, punching her arms up in the air and then clapping her hands. "We get to go on a vacation!"

"A vacation?" I said.

"Yes, I rented a houseboat at Lake Don Pedro, and the girls are all coming with us! Isn't that exciting?" my mom said.

I remembered Lake Don Pedro. We'd gone there right after my mom and Chip had gotten married. It was perfect, actually, with smooth, tan, rolling hills reflected in the glassy blue water under a cloudless sky that went on as far as the eye could see. I took a deep breath. It felt like I was breathing air for the first time, it was so light and easy.

"Wow!" I said, not believing what was happening. It still felt like some bizarre dream. Could this be happening? Was I waking up?

forty-eight

It looked like the cosmetics section of CVS had exploded in our dorm room at Cal State Long Beach. We were almost an hour in with our primping. I turned to face my roommate, Charlotte, with the curling iron still in my hair. Nervous about going on the blind date she was setting me up on, I asked her for the hundredth time, "What's he like? Have you met him? What does he look like?"

"Ugh! Lindsay, I already told you, I only met him once. I think he's nice. I mean, he actually looked at my face instead of my boobs. I can't really remember. He's tall-ish, I think, or maybe that was the other guy. I don't know. Even if he ends up being a troll, at least we will be there together. It'll be fun!"

"Fine, you're right. It will be fun. Besides, I've never been to a party in Beverly Hills," I said, setting down my curling iron. "What should I wear?" I asked, holding up two dresses. I had a black one in my right hand and a white one in my left. I hoped she would choose the black one.

"Umm, they said it was a semi-formal fraternity party, not a funeral. Wear the white one."

I had been afraid she would pick that one—it was the dress I'd worn to our high school graduation just three months earlier, right before I'd broken up with Collin. She was right, though, it was the perfect choice, not too short or revealing, just fitted enough to look polished. I figured I could create some new memories in this dress to go along with my new life and the decision I'd made over the summer.

I'd decided to let everything go: my lunatic of a father, my shame over Adam's death, my failed friendship with Maeve, my abusive boyfriend. I decided to be okay. I decided to not let anyone treat me badly anymore. It was like I'd woken up from a dream, and that hadn't really been my life. Here I was, a high school graduate, young and free, with my whole life ahead of me.

I remembered when I was sunbathing on top of the houseboat my mom and Chip had rented. It was the last day of my "intervention" trip. Lainey, Anna, and Jess were all down on the main deck. I snuck away to be alone for a while. I realized I was tired of worrying what people thought about me. I just wanted to live my life and be myself. I needed to make sure I was happy. I needed to live without the drama—it was exhausting. I needed to clear my head of my toxic thoughts. I went up on the deck high above the water swirling below. It was sunny, but there was a cold breeze, and my beach towel billowed behind me. I pulled it tighter around my shoulders and sat cross-legged on a lounge chair. There was no one up there but me. There was no one to see me cry, no one to tell me what to do, no one to rescue me if I fell.

I realized I was the only one who could save myself. Only I could decide how I let people treat me. Only I could walk away. Only I could let go of the pain. I knew that I needed to be stronger. I knew that I needed to say goodbye to toxic people. I knew that I didn't need to feel bad for them. I knew that I didn't need to feel anything for them at all. I needed to feel for myself. The abusive father, the abusive friend, the abusive boyfriend—I felt nothing for them anymore. I was moving on. I was feeling for myself. I was stronger. I was kind to myself. I was accepting of myself. I was freeing myself.

I wiped the tears from my face. I reached into the pocket of my shorts and felt the jagged stone. I pulled it out and examined its edges and how its sparkles flaked off in my hand. It was fool's gold, not real gold. I'd picked it up when I was ten years old on that fieldtrip to the Empire Mine. I'd thought it was lucky. I'd thought it would protect me. Maybe it had. Maybe it had kept me from being completely swallowed up by the people whom I was allowing to punish me. I'd thought if I kept it, it would turn into gold, but I had been wrong—the gold was within me.

It was mine, and no one could take it from me. I took one more look at the stone, and then I hurled it into the water and watched it disappear. I didn't need it anymore. I was free.

I lifted myself up from the lounge chair, wiped the flakes from my hands, and walked away. I left everything there.

"You're right," I said as I tossed the black dress on my bed. I turned toward the mirror, holding the white dress to my chest. "This is the perfect dress for tonight."

Epilogue

1994

The scent of pink roses lingered in the air as I took the silver kiddush cup from the man who, in just five minutes, would be my husband. I looked into his blue-green eyes as I sipped the sweet wine—eyes that felt like home, eyes that held the promise of every version of myself I had yet to become. In that moment, I felt the world tilt gently forward, carrying me toward a future filled with love and the freedom to be exactly who I am.

Four years ago, when I slipped into that white cocktail dress, I never could have imagined it would lead me here—standing beneath a chuppah in a gown of white, surrounded by family and friends whose laughter and joy seemed to float in the air around us. I never could have imagined meeting someone who was the perfect blend of wit and warmth, strength and tenderness. I didn't know happiness could feel like this—quiet and certain, like something that had always been waiting for me.

It took time for me to believe it, even though I knew from the first moment I saw him—standing on the doorstep of his run-down college apartment—that something had shifted. The night air was cool, the world unremarkable, except for the way he looked at me. And in that look, I felt it for the first time. I was safe.

Acknowledgements

I would like to thank my writing teacher, Carolyn Zeal, for teaching me how to write like I talk so I could tell my story.

I would also like to thank all of my friends, family, and aquaintances who agreed to read my manuscript and provide me with great feedback. The list is long and I am eternally greatful for the time they took out of their busy lives to read my story. Their feedback gave me the courage to publish this story that needed to be told:

Lauren Woomer
Alexandra Nuttall-Smith
Carol Adler
Irina Taylor
Ava Elias
Sara Pacheco
Sabrina Wright-Hobart
Diane Akins

And finally, I would like to thank my mother and my husband. They both have helped me see clearly what a healthy relationship is supposed to look like.

Red Flags to Avoid when starting a new relationship:

1. He gets jealous when you want to spend time with friends or family.

2. He tells you that if you really cared about him, you would want to spend all of your time with him.

3. He has to know where you are at all times.

4. He seems extremely sweet one minute and then completely angry the next.

5. His anger is not proportial to the situation, he over reacts and then appologizes.

6. He gets upset if you don't want to do what he wants to do.

If any of these things happen when you are just starting out in the relationship and they make you feel uncomfortable, leave the relationship. It doesn't get better, it only gets more intense.

Resource guide for getting help:

National Hotline for Domestic Violence – 800-799-7233 or text START to 88788